Lady ✈ MacGyver

CAPTAIN MICHELLE HUNTINGTON

Unbelievable stories with altitude

Copyright©Michelle Huntington 2025
michellehuntington.com
Print ISBN: 978-1-76109-919-9
Ebook ISBN: 978-1-76109-920-5
Typsetting & Design by Rack and Rune Publishing
rackandrune.com
First published 2025 by
GINNINDERRA PRESS
PO Box 2 Bentleigh 3204
ginninderrapress.com.au

Foreword

Most people walk a path lined with tradition and expectations, speaking only when it's easy, seeking guarantees before taking action, and preferring the smoothest road to reach their goals. Others, like Michelle Huntington, meet life head-on, understanding that preparation, experience, and persistence aren't just tools for success—they are tools for survival. For everything else, they adapt as they go. It is no exaggeration to say that Michelle truly is *Lady MacGyver* incarnate. She lives her life as a capable, resourceful leader, always finding a way forward.

For me, this memoir resonates deeply. From different corners of the world, Michelle and I have shared parallel journeys—pursuing the same career with passion. Her stories throughout this book are both captivating and thought-provoking. Her legacy is built on first saying 'yes'—and then figuring out the 'how'.

Michelle's determination to accumulate flight hours by ferrying aircraft across the Pacific was met with scepticism and concern. Still, as a single mother, she took every precaution to ensure a safe return. She understood that foresight, study, and preparation mean more than safety—lives are literally at stake. And those lives, the ones we carry across the globe, matter far more than any bottom line.

Dr. Tony Kern, CEO of Convergent Performance, once asked what could be done to improve aviation safety for the next generation of pilots. Today, my answer is 'give them this book!'.

Within these pages lie lessons on preparation, accountability, self-discipline, and the value of questioning what's easy. Michelle's example teaches future aviators the importance of saying 'no' and walking away when safety or ethics demand it. As she puts it, 'Safety is about lives.'

You'll read how Michelle remained calm and capable after a lightning strike disabled her aircraft's systems mid-flight. She shares stories of navigating not only technical crises but also human ones—facing fear, unchecked egos, interpersonal challenges, and those who crossed both professional and personal boundaries. She shows courage in removing a crew member who reported to duty impaired, in diverting a flight with unruly passengers, in challenging fuel miscalculations, and intervening when cabin crew were undermined.

Being a woman in aviation during those early days wasn't easy for any of us. But Michelle met every challenge with grit, humour, and professionalism. Each decision she made, and every obstacle she faced, offers a perspective worth studying.

While raising a teenager, expecting twins, and managing a life-changing health diagnosis, Michelle not only survived—she continued to thrive. Returning to the skies, she was promoted to Captain. So when boundaries were crossed in unacceptable ways, her response was swift, professional and resolute. Unwilling to have the matter swept aside, Michelle took a principled stand, only to find her career shifting irrevocably.

But through every upheaval—from career, to health, to finances, to facing down workplace misogyny—Michelle's story proves one thing: as long as we're breathing, our story will change and evolve. For future pilots Lady MacGyver offers vital insights and life lessons, and for those who remember aviation's golden

days, moments of sheer delight; but most importantly, for anyone and everyone who has ever faced life's hardest tests, Captain Huntingon's laugh-out-loud humour and unflinching courage is utterly inspirational. So buckle up, readers—you're in for one hell of a ride!

Karlene K. Petitt, PhD, MBA, MHS
Retired Delta Captain

*Typed: A350, A330, B777,
B747-400, B747, B767,
B757, B737, B727*

For Guy x

Contents

Preface	11
Acknowledgements	13
Glossary of Terms	14
Introduction	21

Part 1 - Pre Flight

Age 7—Fighter Pilot	25
Giraffe on Roller Skates	27
Tampons to Stop Your Guts Falling Out	29
Archaeology and Guns	31
Welding and Pearls	33
BAFTA. No Tampon.	35
Bank Says No	37

Part 2 - Learning to Fly

Vomit Down Your Shirt	41
Hours	45
HUET	49
No Pants Required	53
Lady MacGyver	64
Miss Identify	67
Testing Times	69
Woman's First Flight	73

Part 3 - Instructor

Take off Power	78
Lost 3,000 Feet Doing a Wee	81
Following the Magenta Line	85
Grade 2 Dickhead	87
Four Private Pilots Lost	89
CEO Mentality	91

Part 4 - Corporate Pilot

Mayday Mayday! 6 Souls Onboard	95
Lake Cargelligo	97
FO or FA?	101
We Want a Man	102
Ad Man & Cheese	104
Bottle of Urine at My Head	107
Flying Angels	109
Lightning is Scary	111
Rex Interview	116

Part 5 - REX First Officer
Pilot Crash Pad	121
One of the Boys	124
Victor the Trickster	126
Captain, my Captain	130

Part 6 - Rex Captain
Drunk FO	135
Sunshine Every Day	139
Losing My Virginity to Richard Branson	141

Part 7 - Virgin First Officer
eMpTy	145
Captain, Order Me a Tea, Please?	150
Dissent and Violating Safety	153
Ladies of the Flight	161
Cat in The Overhead Locker	162
Left Over In A Hotel	163
SAM	165
Human Factors	168
UFO or UAV?	171
What a Bitch	173
I Would Look Better in That Uniform	175
Twins and Wheels	176
Cancerous Interruptus	178
Another Empty Kitchen	186
Gluten Air Tolerance	194
Keenly-Huntingcock and Melon Boobs	196
Weird Captain	200

Part 8 - Virgin Captain
I Made Magda Cry	204
Fangirl	206
I Turn Left	209
PILC	211
Karen in Row 3	214
Risk 185 or Save 1?	216
Innuendos	220
Grabbed from Behind	222
Boys Will Be Boys	225

Part 9 - Flying Away
Flying Away	231
Epilogue	234

Part 5 - REX First Officer
Pilot Crash Pad	121
One of the Boys	124
Victor the Trickster	126
Captain, my Captain	130

Part 6 - Rex Captain
Drunk FO	135
Sunshine Every Day	139
Losing My Virginity to Richard Branson	141

Part 7 - Virgin First Officer
eMpTy	145
Captain, Order Me a Tea, Please?	150
Dissent and Violating Safety	153
Ladies of the Flight	161
Cat in The Overhead Locker	162
Left Over In A Hotel	163
SAM	165
Human Factors	168
UFO or UAV?	171
What a Bitch	173
I Would Look Better in That Uniform	175
Twins and Wheels	176
Cancerous Interruptus	178
Another Empty Kitchen	186
Gluten Air Tolerance	194
Keenly-Huntingcock and Melon Boobs	196
Weird Captain	200

Part 8 - Virgin Captain
I Made Magda Cry	204
Fangirl	206
I Turn Left	209
PILC	211
Karen in Row 3	214
Risk 185 or Save 1?	216
Innuendos	220
Grabbed from Behind	222
Boys Will Be Boys	225

Part 9 - Flying Away
Flying Away	231
Epilogue	234

Preface

This book is a collection of my aviation stories that I was encouraged to share. When you tell your stories to people and, at first, they can't believe they are actually *true*, then 'demand' you put them into a book, you start to listen.

I had so much fun during my flying career, and, of course, there were also some challenges. Aviation is still a male-dominated industry but there are plenty of us women who would describe ourselves as ′Aerosexual′.

The Urban Dictionary defines Aerosexual as:

A person having an avid love and sexual desire of aircraft beyond the average person's interest. They openly admit their love of aviation and all things air- related.

That would probably describe me, and most of the pilots I know.

I am one to look up overhead every time I hear an aircraft engine. I instantly try and determine the engine make, the altitude, and model of aircraft.

I love the smell of Jet A1 (fuel). I think this comes from my childhood when we had kerosene heaters. That smell reminds me of going out to the airport as a child, with Dad, and being around aircraft. That smell usually meant going up in the air, or holidays. It's a sensory thing.

When I would do walkarounds, checking the exterior of the plane, the tail pipe of the engine would still be smoking; it's highly toxic, but most of us (okay, some of us) aerosexual pilots would have a big whiff as we went past.

Captain Michelle Huntington

We talk about aircraft all the time.
By the way, how do you know there's a pilot in the room?
Oh, they tell you! (and they always have the biggest watches)
Enjoy

Acknowledgements

To Guy—my muse, strength, husband, and lover—thank you for your unwavering support and encouragement in bringing these stories to life. Our morning coffee chats on the front porch remain my most treasured moments of each day.

Thank you Tom, for being my co-pilot. I'm deeply grateful to Maddie, Jack, and Jasper for their patience through countless edits and dinner table discussions. Special thanks to my mum, who read and edited these stories whilst bravely managing her emotional responses to tales she had never heard before.

To Debbie and Mandy, whose steady guidance made the publishing journey both seamless and delightful—your support has been invaluable.

Sarah, your wisdom and mentoring transformed these pages into a cohesive book. Your mastery brought both polish and joy to the editing journey.

Tahlia, your fresh perspective and keen eye for detail brought welcome insights to these pages.

My heartfelt appreciation extends to all the readers who have shared how these stories helped them see their own experiences in a new light. Your feedback has given this work its deepest meaning.

Glossary of Terms

AGL (Above Ground Level) — The vertical distance measured between the aircraft and a specific land mass.

AMSL (Above Mean Sea Level) — The vertical distance measured between the aircraft and the average level of the Earth's oceans.

Aileron — The movable, hinged flight control surfaces that are used in pairs with opposite motions to control the roll of an aircraft.

Airline — A company or organisation that offers regularly scheduled flights and routes.

Airspace Classes — The different types of airspace defined by the International Civil Aviation Organisation (ICAO) and adopted around the world. They include controlled, uncontrolled, and special use airspace.

Altimeter — An instrument that measures an object's altitude above a fixed surface.

Altitude Indicator — An instrument that indicates aircraft orientation relative to the earth's horizon.

Angle of Attack — The angle between a reference line on an aerofoil and the direction of the oncoming air.

Approach — The phase of flight when the pilot intends to land on the runway. There are different types of approaches, depending on whether the pilot is flying VFR or IFR.

Apron/Tarmac — The paved area at an airport where aircraft park, fuel, load, and unload.

ATC (Air Traffic Control) — A ground-based service that ensures safety of air traffic by directing aircraft in the area during take-off, landing, and while flying in the designated airspace.

ATIS (Automatic Terminal Information Service) — A continuous broadcast of pre-recorded aviation information available to pilots around specific terminals. The information is constantly updated and designed for mass spreading of relevant information, which is particularly useful at busy airports.

ATPL — Air transport pilot licence.

Base Leg — The flight path in an airport pattern that runs in the runway landing direction.

Cabin Service Manager (CSM) / Cabin Supervisor (CS) — The cabin crew member responsible for management of the cabin crew and passengers. The CSM is the most senior person in the aircraft, after the pilots.

Captain (Capt.) — A pilot who is qualified to command the aircraft. The captain of a commercial aircraft will have many aviation licences, aircraft endorsements and will be approved by the airline company to operate on airline services. The captain occupies the left seat in commercial fixed wing aircraft.

CASA (Civil Aviation Safety Authority) — Government body that regulates Australian aviation safety, including licensing of pilots and aircraft registration.

CFI — Chief Flying Instructor.

Charter — The business of renting all seats on an aircraft rather than a commercial flight where seats are sold individually.

CIR (Command Instrument Rating) — The qualification to fly as pilot in command in IFR flight.

Class D airspace — The controlled airspace that surrounds general aviation, and regional airports equipped with a control tower. There are Class A to Class G airspaces.

Clearance — The authorisation provided by air traffic control for aircraft to proceed with a particular action in controlled airspace, which is designed to prevent aircraft collisions.

Climb — The act of increasing aircraft altitude, typically to a designated level.

Cockpit — The cockpit of a plane is located at the front. It contains the instrument panel and pilots' seats.

Contrail — A streak of condensed water vapor in the air due to the heat produced by aircraft engines at high altitudes.

Chemtrail — See above ;)

Controlled Airspace — Designated airspace within which Air Traffic Control provides aircraft movement instructions and regulations.

CPL — Commercial pilot licence.

Crosswind — Wind that is blowing perpendicular to the aircraft course.

Descent — The act of decreasing aircraft altitude, typically to a designated level.

Downwind Leg — A flight path parallel to, but running the opposite direction of, the runway intended for landing.

ETA (Estimated Time of Arrival) — The time you will arrive at a destination, based on the local time.

ETD (Estimated Time of Departure) — The time you plan to depart, based on the local time.

Ferry Flight — A flight intended to return an aircraft to base; deliver a new aircraft from the manufacturer to the purchaser; move an aircraft from one operations base to another; or move an aircraft for the purpose of maintenance.

Final Approach — A flight path running in the direction of the runway intended for landing that ends with a landing.

Firewall — A fire-resistant bulkhead that is situated between the engine and other aircraft areas.

First Officer (FO) — The Co-Pilot, second-in-command. The FO occupies the right seat in commercial fixed wing aircraft.

Flaps — Flaps are a kind of high-lift device used to increase the lift of an aircraft wing at a given airspeed. They are flat devices, typically located on the edges of an aircraft wing, that control lift at specific speeds.

Flare — A manoeuvre that typically occurs during the landing stage of an aircraft. The aircraft nose is pointed upwards, which lowers the descent rate in preparation for landing.

Flight Deck — An area at the front of the airplane where the pilot and aircraft controls are situated; in other words, the cockpit.

Flight Plan — Formatted information provided by pilots or dispatchers regarding an upcoming flight, including details such as destination, path, timing, etc.

Flying Dirty — Flying with extendable surfaces in their extended states to create drag, such as flaps extended and landing gear out.

Fog — Fog is a thick cloud of tiny water droplets at or near the Earth's surface that obscures visibility.

General Aviation — The division of civil aviation aircraft operations that includes all but commercial air transport and aerial work.

General Aviation Aerodrome Procedures (GAAP) — A (now retired) class of airspace where pilots were responsible for their own separation from other aircraft, with a control tower to give take-off and landing clearances only.

Go-Around — A go-around occurs when the pilot abandons a landing and goes around the flight pattern before attempting to land.

Hangar — A building made to hold aircraft for storing, maintenance, assembly, etc.

IFR (Instrument Flight Rules) — Regulations that define aircraft operations when pilots are not able to operate using visual references.

IFR Reporting Point — A position either over a ground-based Navaid or a GPS waypoint, where position reporting is required, or can act as a turning point

ILS (Instrument Landing System) — A ground-based system that provides directional information for aircraft attempting to land in low visibility situations.

IMC (Instrument Meteorological Conditions) — Weather conditions that cause a situation where pilots are not able to operate using visual references.

Jet — An aircraft propelled by one or more jet engines.

Knot — A measurement of speed referenced by nautical miles: 1 knot = 1 nautical mile per hour = 1.852 km/hour.

Magneto — An aircraft engine component that generates high voltage to ignite spark plugs.

Minimum Crew — The minimum crew for a Boeing 737 is two pilots (pilot and co-pilot).

MTOW — Maximum Take-Off Weight.

NAVAID — Navigation Aid.

NDB (Non-Directional Beacon) — is a radio transmitter at a known location used as a navigation aid.

Operating Limitations — Restrictions defined by an aircraft manufacturer including airspeed, weight, etc.

Overshoot — Landing aircraft beyond (past) the runway.

PIC (Pilot-In-Command) — The designated person aboard the aircraft who is responsible under the regulations for the safety of all persons during flight. The PIC has final authority as to the disposition of the aircraft and for discipline for all persons on board.

PPL (Private Pilot Licence) — Required to fly any CASA-registered aircraft.

Propeller — A piece of aircraft equipment that contains rotating blades, creating engine thrust.

Roll — Aircraft rotation along the longitudinal axis, which runs from the nose to tail.

Rudder — An aircraft surface used to control the yaw movement.

RWY (Runway) — A defined rectangular area on a land airport prepared for the landing and take-off of aircraft.

Straight-and-Level Flight — Maintaining a consistent heading and altitude during flight.

Tarmac — The paved area at an airport where aircraft park, fuel, load, and unload.

Threshold — The area of a runway, designated with particular markings, indicating the beginning of a runway.

Throttle — A device that controls the amount of power outputted by the engine.

Touch-and-Go — An aircraft manoeuvre used to practice landing techniques by simply landing on the runway and taking off once more without coming to a full stop.

Upwind Leg — The flight path in an airport pattern that runs parallel to the runway landing direction, along the same direction the aircraft will be landing. (See Downwind Leg).

VFR (Visual Flight Rules) — Regulations that define aircraft operations when pilots are able to operate using visual references.

VMC (Visual Meteorological Conditions) — Weather conditions enabling a situation where pilots are able to operate using visual references.

VOR (Very High Frequency Omni-Directional Range) — A short-range radio aircraft navigation system that allows equipped aircraft to receive directional information through radio signals from ground-based beacons.

Yaw — The movement of an aircraft around the vertical axis, characterised by the nose moving side-to-side. The rudder controls yaw.

Introduction

My journey to becoming an airline captain defied every expectation and shattered countless myths about women in aviation. That childhood dream, sparked by winning a fighter jet ride in a colouring competition, refused to die despite years of being told it was impossible.

While writing this book, I realised my experiences offer vital insights about resilience and authenticity in the face of systemic resistance. When sharing stories from my aviation career - whether about jerry-rigging aircraft across the Pacific or navigating institutionalised sexism - audiences consistently connect with the universal themes beneath the technical details. They recognise their own challenges in my experiences of breaking through barriers and finding innovative solutions under pressure.

This memoir transcends the typical "women in aviation" narrative. It delves into trusting your instincts when conventional wisdom declares failure inevitable. It explores finding creative solutions when standard approaches collapse. Most crucially, it demonstrates maintaining authenticity in environments that demand conformity.

Throughout my career, I have witnessed both the finest and worst aspects of human nature at 35,000 feet. My experiences range from profound kindness from strangers in remote airfields to institutional betrayal from trusted colleagues. Each encounter taught invaluable lessons about leadership, resilience, and the power of unwavering self-belief.

The aviation industry desperately needs diverse voices and perspectives. However, this book reaches beyond inspiring future pilots. Through my story, readers from all backgrounds will discover tools for navigating their own challenging environments, whether that involves breaking into a male-dominated industry, transitioning careers, or confronting any situation that tests their resilience.

My roles as flying instructor, airline captain, cancer survivor, and single mother have provided unique insights into pursuing ambitious dreams, all while maintaining humanity. Now, as a speaker and consultant, I witness how these lessons resonate far beyond the flight deck.

This book arrives at a crucial moment in workplace culture. Organisations are grappling with diversity, authenticity, and institutional change. My story offers both inspiration and practical strategies for anyone working to create more inclusive, innovative environments.

I wrote this book for everyone who has ever been told they do not belong, for those searching for courage to change direction, and for people striving to maintain their authentic selves whilst breaking new ground. If my journey to becoming an airline captain can help others navigate their own transformations with greater confidence and creativity, then sharing these stories - even the painful ones - serves a purpose beyond my personal narrative. So here are my stories.

The sky was never the limit. It was merely the beginning.

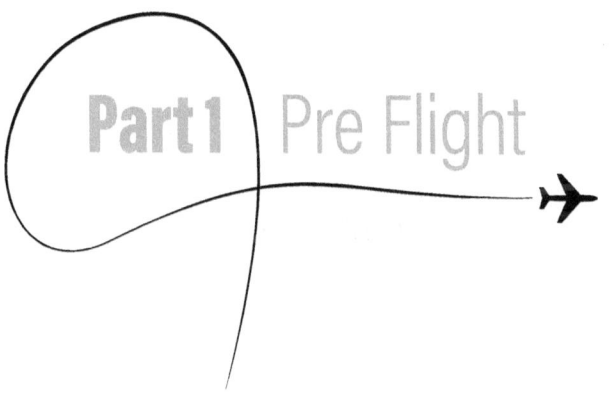

"The moment you doubt whether you can fly, you cease forever to be able to do it" - J M Barrie, Peter Pan

Age 7—Fighter Pilot

At age 7, I had my first flight... in a fighter jet. My dad was an engineer at the RAAF base in Butterworth, Malaysia. To entertain the kids on base they held colouring competitions with prizes that would make any junior aviator's heart soar—flights in real military aircraft! Health and Safety was... let's say, more relaxed back then.

I won flights in a Mirage Fighter, a Caribou, a Chinook, and a Hercules. Not your average carnival rides.

Strapped into the cockpit with a five-point harness, I heard the Captain's stern warning: 'DON'T touch anything!' Solid advice for a 7-year-old.

I was giddy with a blend of excitement and trepidation.

The scent of burnt kerosene filled the air as G-forces thrust me back into my seat. We climbed vertically, pitched over, then experienced weightlessness for what felt like an eternity, though it was only seconds. I screamed all the way back down—not from fear, but from sheer excitement.

Whilst viewing the world from that cockpit, a new dream took flight. *I can do that*, I thought to myself, *I'm going to fly planes*. In my childish naivety, it looked easy.

On the base, pilots were revered like demi-gods. They strode across the tarmac in their flight suits, exuding confidence and cool. I'd watch them as they appeared to effortlessly manoeuvre these machines through the sky.

My parents, ever supportive, told me I'd need to work and study hard. I did.

Fast-forward some 40 years and I'm the Captain of a Boeing 737.

The journey wasn't always smooth. Some called me reckless for how I built my flight hours; others said I took too many risks; a few even tried to clip my wings.

Dreams don't come with an instruction manual, so I just winged it.

Enjoy the flight—I know I do, every single time.

Giraffe on Roller Skates

We moved back to Australia and followed Dad's work to different Airforce bases, this meant five primary schools and two high schools. Dad left the RAAF and worked for Ansett and Qantas. Aviation was all around me, shaping my worldview with every move.

Winging it: Figuring it out as you go.

It was at Newcastle Beach where I, a tall teenage girl with blonde hair and blue eyes, said 'Yes' to something, without having the requisite skill, and truly made a spectacle of myself. I got a job promoting Coca-Cola. I was to wear a *red* bikini, hold a tray of drinks and offer them to passers-by—all on roller skates!

There was a problem. I didn't know how to skate. Imagine a giraffe on roller skates and you would be close to understanding my poise and my dilemma.

Now, most sensible people would have politely declined this potential disaster, but where's the fun in that? I had a tendency, no, a *strong impulse*, to say 'Yes' to every opportunity... and figure it out later. 'Fake it 'till you make it' wasn't just a motto; it was becoming my philosophy of life.

So, there I was, a human giraffe on wheels, clutching onto the railing at the sea front for dear life while smiling like I was having the time of my life. Passersby would approach, interested in a free Coke. I'd summon my steadiest voice and say, 'You'll have to come to me if you want one.'

It wasn't seduction; it was survival.

Looking back, I can't help but laugh at the absurdity of it all. However, that day taught me something invaluable. It taught me that sometimes, the most memorable experiences come from saying 'Yes' to the most ridiculous propositions.

I didn't become a roller-skating champion that day, but I did learn I could face challenges with a smile, even if my knees were shaking and my heart was pounding. It was my first lesson in the art of winging it—a skill that would prove invaluable in my future aviation career. (No pun intended.)

Life's too short to always play it safe. Sometimes, you've got to strap on those metaphorical roller skates, don the red bikini of courage, and glide (or wobble) your way into the unknown.

I'm just glad you don't need to wear roller skates on a plane. I was going to be a pilot, not a skater. The promotional work continued through university, and later when I became a pilot. Every experience I gained, regardless of how unconventional, was preparing me for my journey.

Tampons to Stop Your Guts Falling Out

I was lucky, my parents never said 'No' to my dreams. They supported every childish fantasy my sister and I had. Our little creative minds dreamed Big.

Saying 'Yes' to opportunities created all sorts of adventures; saying 'Yes' also made me highly compliant. I was a good girl. I studied hard while working towards my dream of flying.

In Year 10, I had a routine appointment with the school's Career Advisor. The small windowless office, painted that government 'greige' (grey beige), was the setting where I received my first detour; my first roadblock.

I walked in and sat down. She smiled and said, 'Michelle. What do you want to be when you grow up?' She had clearly asked this rehearsed question a few times that day.

'I want to be a pilot,' I said.

She looked a little quizzical. 'Michelle, women can't be pilots.'

'Why not?' I replied.

'Michelle, women are built differently to men.'

'Yeah.'

'You'll have to wear a tampon every time you fly.'

'What?'

'You know. Otherwise, your guts will fall out.'

It was quite absurd, backward, and utterly disheartening that in the late 1980s, a formal 'guide' for the next generation held such antiquated views.

Due to my compliance, I had always done well; saying 'Yes' to everything and everyone. She went on to tell me that I was good at art, and should go to university or art school and study to become an artist.

In the late 80s it was still an outlandish idea that a woman could become an airline captain. The story of Deborah Lawrie fighting with Ansett for the right to be a pilot hadn't filtered down into the lexicon of career options for girls.

Nobody should let a lack of role models stop them from trying anything, or dreaming Big, but because of my tendency for compliance, I actually gave up my dream of being a pilot, and followed Mrs Middlebrook's advice, I enrolled in a Bachelor's degree in Visual Arts.

I became an exhibiting artist, commissioned to paint large murals and art installations. I love to express myself through paint. Some would say my style is adventurous and abstract.

But my dream didn't die; it went into hibernation. Waiting for the right spark.

It wasn't until I was older that I learned to say 'Yes' —to myself.

Turns out women *can* fly planes—and without their insides escaping! We can even teach others to do the same. Some of my former students are now Captains at Emirates, Qantas, Rex, Virgin, Qatar, JAL, and other international airlines.

Thank you, Mrs M, for doing your best to guide my career. I thank you for the first hurdle that I would need to overcome; the first roadblock that was placed in my path. Your well-meaning but misguided advice didn't clip my wings — it gave them an unexpected coat of paint. Now, when I'm not in the cockpit, I'm wielding a paintbrush, creating abstract masterpieces that capture that same thrill of breaking through clouds and shattering glass ceilings.

Remember, always pack an extra tampon—not for flying, but for those inevitable naysayers who might need to plug up their outdated opinions!

Archaeology and Guns

I never imagined work in Archaeology would result in having a shotgun pointed at my head, but then, my life has never been short on surprises.

After my foray into the world of art, life took another unexpected turn. I fell in love with an Agriculture student and found myself living on a farm, just outside Moree, New South Wales. Suddenly, I was a cotton farmer. It turns out there's a stark contrast between flying planes and watching plants grow.

That Art degree came in handy after all. I landed a job with Yurandali Aboriginal Artist Corporation, teaching traditional techniques to members of the local Kamilaroi community, helping them continue their traditions. I taught contemporary techniques around composition, colours, and colour theory, and my administrative skills helped us secure the contract for the Sydney 2000 Olympic Games bedding artwork.

I became very close to members of the community and noticed an exhibition at the local gallery was displaying sacred Aboriginal artefacts with a severe lack of cultural sensitivity. The director of the gallery had business acumen, however no regard for the sensibility nor sentiment of the Indigenous community.

When the gallery director's position opened up, I thought it was a perfect opportunity to restore cultural respect and traditions and I applied. I didn't get the job, as they deemed me unqualified. They did, however, suggest I study a higher qualification.

The incumbent continued in the role, and I went on to pursue a

Masters in Archaeology, focusing on Indigenous culture, strengthening my chances of the role in the future.

The practical components of my degree became interesting. I was heavily pregnant so at digs I would lie on my side, large belly protruding, while brushing away soil from artefacts. I certainly lacked grace when getting up from these prone positions!

Whilst studying, I became aware that the gallery director role was more political than practical, plus my circumstances had changed. We had left the cotton farm and moved to Narrabri. Here I met some people from the National Parks and Wildlife Service. They offered me a contract job near Walgett, investigating Indigenous artefacts on a farmer's land. A *perfect* opportunity to use my new degree.

A farmer had reported finding some Aboriginal artefacts on his land, which he had unearthed when ploughing his field. He gave me permission to camp on his property in a tent.

After the first day, I sat down around the campfire and prepared dinner. The farmer had gone out to the pub. When he returned, smelling of beer, he walked up to my camp with a shotgun and demanded that I immediately leave his property or he'd shoot me!

'But you've given me permission to be here,' I replied.

'I'm revoking that,' he said. 'Get off my land!'

I asked him, 'Why the change of mind?'

Holding his gun he said, 'I don't want the government taking my land, so get off.'

As I packed up my car, staring down the barrel of his shotgun, I realised two things: Archaeology might not be my calling after all; and my appetite for risk was about to take a whole new direction.

Lady MacGyver

Welding and Pearls

After swapping cotton fields for the 'Big Smoke' of Narrabri (population: 13,000), I found myself teaching at the local TAFE (Technical and Further Education) college. Little did I know, I was about to become their Swiss Army Knife of Education.

Once you're in their system, they utilise you for *every* skill you possibly have. Teachers were hard to come by.

At first, I was employed to teach Art; including printmaking and painting, but they found out about other skills I'd collected along the way. In my Visual Arts degree, I learned welding for sculpture armatures. I'd also worked in hospitality and had some visual merchandising experience at Grace Bros (now Myer), during university breaks.

My eclectic skill set became known at TAFE, and suddenly I wasn't *just* the art teacher—I was Narrabri TAFE's Jack-of-All-Trades! I started teaching artistic welding, making things like fireplace pokers and decorative hooks. Then I moved on to teaching real welding to apprentices, guided by a handbook and the head teacher.

Then, based on my retail experience working in department stores, I started teaching business studies and hospitality.

Sometimes I would be teaching all these different courses in the one day. It was not unusual for me to teach business studies in the morning, wearing heels, stockings, business suit and pearls; then I would go across to welding, change into overalls and a leather apron (always keeping my pearls on); then head over to teach painting or sculpture. My pearls became my signature.

Being a female welding instructor raised a few eyebrows. Some young apprentices thought it was a joke. I would then set out to prove them wrong by sitting down and showing them what I could do. However, my welding had to be *perfect* to gain their respect.

Funny how that works in male-dominated industries. As a woman, you need to be perfect just to be taken seriously. I'm sure all the men hold each other to the same exacting standards...?

Little did these lads know, they were preparing me for the world of aviation. If I could win over sceptical welding apprentices, surely I could handle a few doubtful pilots? After all, whether you're fusing metal or flying planes, it's all about *precision* and proving yourself.

Juggling business suits and welding masks, with pearls gleaming under my protective gear, wasn't quite the career path I'd envisioned, but it was certainly preparing me for a future where adaptability would be my greatest asset.

BAFTA. No Tampon.

After my marriage broke down, my young son and I moved to Tamworth. In a bout of post-divorce rebellion, I dyed my hair black and cut it very short. Regret set in fast. I soon found myself with a beautiful hairdresser, pleading for a return to blonde.

This angel of a stylist didn't just fix my hair—she adopted me into her social circle. Among her friends was the marketing manager at the British Aerospace Flight Training Academy (BAFTA). Before I knew it, I was signing up for their mixed Oz-Tag team.

This new (non-tackling) ball sport provided me with a new social outlet and when I found out what BAFTA was, I became very excited to be surrounded by people involved with aviation. I told my new friend that I'd wanted to fly, but it hadn't worked out.

That first night of Oz-Tag training, I turned up to see one other woman, and a group of men on the 8-player team. I introduced myself, then introduced myself to the other female.

After some small talk, she told me she was a student. Learning to fly. At BAFTA.

My brain short-circuited. A woman? I thought: *How? Why? What?*

I asked her, 'How can you do this?'

She looked surprised but responded, 'Well, you pass the test, you pay the money, and you do the training, it's that easy.'

My mind was whirring. I was told an aviation career was not possible, by my career's counsellor, but here was a woman, about my age, who was learning to fly.

I still can't believe the following words actually left my mouth: 'How do you deal with the tampon thing?'

She looked at me like I'd grown a second head. 'What?'

I wasn't done. I doubled down. 'You know, to stop your guts falling out during flights!'

She blinked, said, 'No,' and walked off, probably wondering if she'd stumbled into a hidden 'Candid Camera' show.

There I stood, realising I'd just regurgitated my Year 10 career advisor's nonsense to a complete (adult) stranger. Top marks for first impressions, Michelle!

This encounter, whilst embarrassing, reignited my dream.

If she can fly, so can I.

I've been asked so many times why I wanted to fly, and I can never articulate it. Flying just lights me up inside. Some loves are hard to explain, they're just *meant to be*.

Bank Says No

Learning to fly is expensive. My dream was back on, but it came with a very hefty price tag, and a significant time commitment.

I decided that I would need a loan; I'd heard of other pilots borrowing money to pay for their lessons.

Working as a TAFE teacher, I didn't see any reason why I *wouldn't* get the loan. I made an appointment with the bank manager, dressed nicely, and completed the extensive paperwork application.

Sitting in his office, I was thinking about the path ahead of me now that my dream was back on. He pulled the application in front of him and started running his finger across the different sections.

'Yes,' his finger moved down the page. 'Yes. Yes.'

The more he moved down the application, the more relief I felt. Then I heard, 'Ummm, no.' He looked up at me and said, 'Women aren't pilots.'

My gender was apparently standing in my way again. I told him that I knew of another woman training to be a pilot at BAFTA; we played Oz-Tag together.

'Well, she must be self-funded,' he retorted, 'we won't fund this.'

I went home dejected and frustrated.

However, I'm now different to my Year 10 self. I still say 'Yes' to opportunity; but I am no longer the compliant girl that allowed others to put roadblocks in her way.

So, I went to another bank. This time I dressed *even more* in line with their narrative, all lashes and lipstick smiles. I told them I wanted to renovate and redecorate my house. They couldn't be more obliging.

I took the bank's money. I sold my house. I sold my car. I moved back in with my mother in Sydney, my young son with me. I went to Bankstown Airport and used all that money to pay upfront for a year of flying lessons.

Nothing was going to stop me now. I was saying a Big 'Yes' to my dreams.

The education system was saying 'No.' The finance industry was saying 'No.'

I was saying 'Yes.'

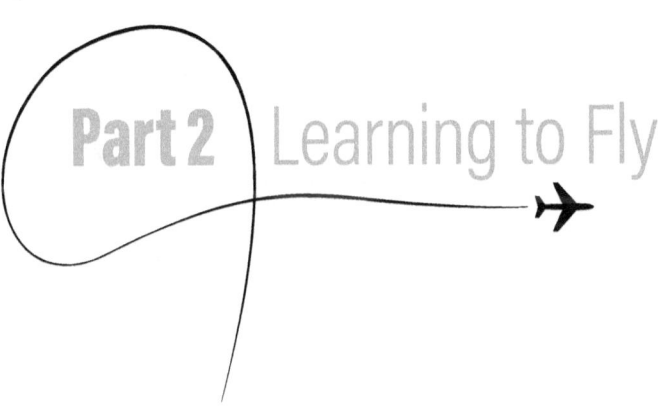

Part 2 Learning to Fly

Lady MacGyver

Vomit Down Your Shirt

My first flying lesson was fast approaching, and I was determined to be fully prepared. I marched into the Pilot Shop at Bankstown, my excitement obvious. They must have seen my naivety a mile off, because I left with an arsenal of pilot gear that would raise an eyebrow on even the most seasoned aviator.

Short sleeve pilot shirts? Check. *Long sleeve ones as well?* Double check. *Clip-on tie for safety, and a regular tie for style*—because options are important when you're about to conquer the skies. *Two-stripe epaulettes, pilot wings*, and *black trousers* completed the official look. But why stop there?

I also snagged a *black flight jacket* with a bright orange satin lining—perfect for those chilly stratospheric temperatures I was surely about to experience. And to commemorate this momentous occasion, I even bought a *sterling silver pearl bracelet* with propeller and wing charms. Oh, and a *framed 747 cockpit poster*, because every aspiring pilot needs inspiration on their bedroom wall, right?

I turned up to my first lesson in full uniform, more pilot-y than any pilot has *ever* piloted before. Striding out onto the tarmac with my crisp ironed shirt and a perfect Windsor knot, I felt invincible. I climbed into the Beagle B.121 Pup, a 1960s British 2 seat single-engine training aircraft.

This was it. I was ready!

We took off in my maiden flight, going through the basics. For 10 glorious minutes, I was living my dream. Then it hit me—nausea like I'd never experienced before. Sweating, stomach churning, mouth-watering. 'I think I'm going to be sick,' I managed to tell my instructor.

'Can you wait till we land? We don't have any sick bags,' he replied, hope clearly evident in his voice.

'I don't think I can wait,' I gulped back.

His solution? 'Then loosen your tie, unbutton your shirt, vomit inside your shirt, then do your shirt back up.'

And that's exactly what I did. My instructor leaned over and moved my microphone to the side, possibly to avoid hearing my breakfast escape in stereo through his headphones.

I rebuttoned my shirt, adjusted my tie, and completed the lesson. It was the last time I would wear that tie. Not because of the breakfast splatter; they can be dangerous in an emergency. It was clip-ons from now on; you'll never be strangled by a clip-on.

That night, I recounted my adventure to my mum. Little did I know, she'd take this nugget of wisdom to heart. Years later, in a glider experience, she told the pilot she was feeling ill. He said he would get her a sick bag, to which she proudly informed her pilot, 'No, no. I know what to do. My daughter is a pilot.'

I can only imagine the pilot's face as she proceeded to vomit down her shirt. At least I was *inspiring* others—even if not quite in the *way* I'd imagined!

After that first lesson, panic set in. I had a moment of stark realization— I'd sold my house, borrowed money to renovate my (now non-existent) house, and sold my car—all to follow my dream. I had paid upfront for a whole year of flying lessons, with no financial parachute. I was a single mother with a 2-year-old making big commitments with my future.

The next day was my second lesson. I hadn't slept well, worrying about what was going to happen. I turned up early to Bankstown Airport and met the same instructor for a 6am start.

We did the pre-brief, which I didn't really listen to, because I was already mentally flying in the training area, thinking about *not vomiting*.

He told me we would be straight and level in this lesson. 'An "easy" flight,' he said.

We took off and I started to get that queasy feeling immediately during the take-off climb. *Crap,* I thought to myself, repeating in my head, *don't throw up, don't throw up.*

This time, my instructor came prepared with a few sick bags. It wasn't long before I used one. This time I moved my mic out of the way whilst he opened vents and looked out the other window. As a junior instructor, I'm sure he hadn't signed up for this.

Feeling ashamed and nauseous, we flew back to the airport.

Determined to beat this, I went for my third lesson on the same day. I spent 10 minutes in the bathroom, washing my face and giving myself a pep talk.

'Toughen up,' I told my reflection. 'This is your dream!'

I walked out taking big breaths, ready to face the sky again.

The day had got warmer and windier.

The whole flying school, mostly young men, had come out to 'support me' before my third flight.

My instructor asked, did I really want to go up again today? I was steadfast. 'Yes. Let's go.'

We took off and got to the training area where I ceremoniously vomited *again*. Defeated, I told him we needed to go back. I sat in the aircraft with my head hanging low, thinking *What have I done? Is this really the career for me?*

The owner of the flight school, also the Chief Flying Instructor (CFI), came out. He hopped into the aircraft and asked, 'How are you going?'

I didn't want to cry, but I couldn't stop it.

'I think I have made a mistake,' I whispered between bouts of tears.

He turned to me and delivered what was to become my life's mantra. 'Michelle, just keep going until you can't.'

He suggested my airsickness might be due to a feeling of a lack of control and fear of the unknown. His solution? Study the next lesson, on turning, and brief him on it the next day. I was to talk him through it as he demonstrated the manoeuvre during the flight.

The next day, I did as he suggested. I briefed him before we flew and talked him through the manoeuvres as he demonstrated them. Suddenly, I was the *teacher*, not just the *student*.

And finally, no vomit!

I took a valuable lesson from this. Anything that stood in my way, I'd tackle as if I had to *teach* it to someone else. Once I understood it well enough to teach it, I'd overcome it.

From that point on, my path to becoming a private pilot was vomit-free.

As I progressed through my training, that first day's experience became a funny anecdote rather than a source of shame. It taught me that resilience isn't about avoiding mistakes or embarrassment. It's about facing that embarrassment, cleaning yourself up, and showing up again the next day. As long as you keep going until you can't, you'll find your way to the skies.

Hours

I now had my private Pilot's Licence with the goal to become a commercial pilot. The minimum requirement was 150 hours, 50 of which needed to be Pilot in Command (not under instruction), to get your commercial licence.

It was time to get creative.

I could've played it safe: hired a plane, circled Bankstown a few hundred times. Or maybe spiced it up with parachute jumping (staying in the plane, mind you), scenic flights, fish spotting, or even mustering stock, but where's the fun in that?

I chose ferry flying, because nothing says ´sensible career progression´ like flying tiny planes across vast oceans when you've barely mastered the local circuit. People often buy small planes from overseas and instead of shipping them back to Australia, they get pilots eager to build hours to fly them back. It's like a transcontinental delivery service, but with more turbulence (and less pizza).

I decided this would be the fastest path to my goal, but I needed guidance. My first ferry flight was with an experienced ferry pilot who was to 'show me the ropes'. The flight we took on was from Ardmore, just below Auckland in New Zealand, back to Sydney.

It was a little Piper Cherokee 140hp slab wing with 4 seats.

The pilot taught me all the little tricks along the way. We had a top ground speed of 60 knots in a plane that had only a small range, so we placed a 44-gallon drum on the back seat with a garden hose connecting the drum to a hand pump on the floor. I was told these are called Christian pumps, after the man that invented them, although I did pray a little as we pumped the fuel out of the drum, into the wing. The hose went into the filler cap on the front of the wing, so it wasn't very aerodynamic.

We took off from Ardmore, made a quick 7-minute hop to Auckland to clear customs, then sneaked north for a cheeky fuel top-up.

Our first stop was to be Norfolk Island, 1,440km away. As we set off, my mentor started dropping pearls of wisdom: 'Only fly during daylight hours, never fly at night, and pick your weather.' Sage advice, considering my experience was limited to the training area around Bankstown, with a few navigation exercises thrown in.

I'm now flying a plane I'm not familiar with, over the Pacific Ocean, albeit with an experienced pilot to guide me.

We started at 6,500ft but ended up skimming the ocean at 500ft (150m) above the waves because the winds were stronger than forecast. The moisture was quite high, and flying at that speed and altitude, you can get carby icing. Ice forming in the carburettor, which makes the engine splutter and can ultimately starve the engine of fuel.

It's amazing how quickly your rectum can pucker when you're that close to the ocean.

Every engine splutter had me doing carby icing checks and involuntary clenching of my buttocks (and everywhere else in my body). It felt like I didn't take a breath for the entire 5.5-hour flight. I was redirecting heat into the fuel line continuously. When we landed on Norfolk Island, I could've cracked walnuts with my buttocks.

The island is higher than the altitude we were flying, so we needed to climb up to land.

The next day, we island-hopped to Lord Howe, a quick 5-hour jaunt. Then finally, the home stretch—about 3 hours from Lord Howe to Kempsey, a trip that twin-engine aircraft do in less than half the time.

Mission accomplished; sphincter unclenched.

Back at the flying school, fate decided to test my newfound bravery. An airport regular came in, asking who wanted to fly his newly purchased plane. Every pilot present said a big 'Yes!'

'There's a catch,' he added. 'It's in Arizona and you would need to fly it back here.' This time I was the only one who said, 'Yes,' — the other pilots were thinking this was crazy.

I had volunteered to fly a small single engine aircraft, about the size of a Hyundai Getz, with wings, from the USA to Australia, across the Pacific. Solo. Apparently, my sense of self-preservation had gone AWOL.

As reality sank in, even I questioned my sanity. My instructor helpfully suggested I build hours 'like everyone else,' in the safety of familiar airspace. But where's the story in that? Fly north, keep Australia on the left; fly south, keep Australia on the right. Rinse and repeat. Boring!

The suspenseful experience flying from New Zealand was still fresh in my mind. I needed more preparation. After all, I was about to fly a *lot* further, across longer stretches of the Pacific.

My instructor reminded me, it was very different to the type of flying I had done so far. He pointed out all the risks and why I *shouldn't* do it. I'd also heard a harrowing story of another ferry pilot, Ray Clamback, who'd ditched in the Pacific.

The version of the story I heard was a masterpiece of Aussie embellishment—axes, life rafts, and rectums absorbing seawater! Most of it untrue of course, but the story had set my mind racing with fear.

The real story? Ray was ferrying a new Cherokee Archer from Florida to Hilo, Hawaii, with his customer, Shane, a doctor who'd purchased the plane. Over the Pacific, they noticed falling oil pressure, increasing engine temperature, and eventually experienced engine failure. They had to ditch in the water.

The US Coast Guard had been notified, but lost them after they experienced a loss of electrics. No radio, no landing lights to see the water, no outside lights for the Coast Guard to see. Just two men, a plane, and a whole lot of ocean.

Swallowing saltwater is bad news, and Shane, being a doctor, kept encouraging Ray to vomit. (*Swallowed*—not absorbed up the rectum as I was told). The US Coast Guard came to the rescue, proving once again that they're the real MVPs (most valuable players) of the seas.

Ray, being the persistent (or crazy) pilot he was, ditched two more times. Why stop at one near-death experience when you can have three? You can read about his experiences online, but trust me, the Aussie grapevine version is much more entertaining!

Learning about Ray's adventures was a wake-up call. If I was going to potentially crash into the ocean, I might as well be prepared. So, I did what any sensible person would do: I signed up for Helicopter Underwater Escape Training (HUET). If I was to ditch in the Pacific, I wanted to increase my chances of survival.

As I prepared for my solo adventure, I couldn't help but wonder: *Was I brave, crazy, or just really, really bad at saying 'No' to challenges?* Only time (and possibly the Pacific Ocean) would tell.

One thing was certain: my journey to becoming a commercial pilot was going to be *anything* but boring. Bring on the adventure, the challenges, and hopefully, a lot less vomit than Ray experienced. What's life without a little (or a lot) of risk?

HUET

All that thinking about ferrying small aircraft over *much* longer distances than New Zealand to Australia, coupled with the stories of pilots ditching in the water, was causing me some anxiety.

The body-clenching experience from New Zealand was fresh in my mind, and I wondered if I could survive such physical tension all the way from America.

I knew HUET training would help alleviate the anxiety. It would make me feel more prepared if something *did* go wrong over the Pacific. Helicopter Underwater Escape Training (HUET) teaches you what to do, and how to survive, if you ditch in the ocean. I would be in a small plane, not a helicopter, but it is the same dilemma.

I enrolled in HUET at the Naval Base in Nowra. It was the only place at the time offering training to civilians.

As a strong swimmer, I hadn't considered how hard it could be.

After signing enough waivers to paper a small country, I found myself in an indoor pool. I had my swimmers on and was instructed to put on overalls and a life jacket that goes around your neck. They're designed for helicopters, but they make sense for long periods of plane flying too, as they are comfortable, and don't get in the way of the seat, seatbelt, or moving around the cockpit.

During the briefing, we were told what would happen, how we would feel, and how the panic would set in. I have always prided myself on being quite a logical thinker, but we were told that under duress, in the dark, underwater, with the fear of the unknown, that logical thinking would leave us. That is exactly what happened.

The dry run on land was easy. I was the picture of calm competence. We were told how long to hold our breath and what our actions would be. It all seemed clear and reasonable. In the water, everything changed.

In the pool, confidently sitting in the cockpit, I was prepared for what was about to happen. The water started to rise over my feet. We were to hold our breath when the water reached our neck; it went from my waist to over my head much quicker than I expected; I panicked. Adrenaline flooded my body, and my anxiety was maxing out. I knew there were divers there to assist; to pull me up very quickly if needed; but that didn't stop the extreme panic.

The window was open and all I had to do was swim out. Simple, right? I held my breath, and my lungs began to burn, feeling like they would explode from the pressure. Feeling like minutes, yet just on 30 seconds, I let some air bubbles escape my mouth, having an almost out of body experience watching them travel upwards and then worrying I had released too much air, and I'd run out. I did eventually swim out, but the panic!

The next scenario was with the cockpit window closed; we had to open the door against the force of water. This is more like a small plane where you can't open the window anyway.

We practiced opening the door as the water was rising, where the resistance made it very difficult. We then practiced opening the door fully submerged, allowing the pressure inside the cabin to equalize, whilst holding our breath throughout.

The experience up until this point had been with calm water, assuming a smooth landing.

They then stepped up the intensity.

The ocean is rarely going to pause its churning whilst you land your stricken little plane. The pool waves were added to the challenge, plus rain, and then they turned off the lights.

They stepped up the simulation to also include tumbling on landing, which is the more likely scenario.

The cockpit was lowered into the water, tumbling like a washing machine so now I was upside down, waves crashing, rain pelting, darkness everywhere. Water rising. Complete disorientation. Terrifying. Extreme Panic. No logical thoughts were available even though we were told what to do prior.

Without a doubt, the scariest, most extreme experience I have *ever* had.

I had to do it twice; apparently once wasn't traumatic enough.

The second time, I forced myself to follow the process. I had to trust what they told me. After the tumbling stopped, I undid the seatbelt and let myself float. Your lungs are filled with air and will naturally pull you towards the surface. Whilst floating, I simply followed that buoyancy to find the exit above.

Pro tip: if you orientate to the exit that's down, you're in for a bad time.

I was happier with the outcome of the second practice. We did a few more scenarios with added difficulties. I was learning to turn off the fear response in my brain. I could follow the procedure and save myself; or maybe my brain just gave up. Either way, I was *not* drowning.

I am very grateful for this training. Had I faced this scenario *without* this training, I am sure I would not be writing this story for you.

The training was incredibly helpful, but then the nightmares started. I was now thinking about all the 'what ifs'. I was 28, and a single mum of a 2-year-old son. The gravity of it all hit home about a week before I left for the USA to fly this small plane back to Australia. My anxiety had reached its peak; deciding to ignore it, I kept saying to myself, 'Keep going till you can't, Michelle'.

I was ready to take on the Pacific in a flying tin can, armed with nothing but my wits, a heap of anxiety, and the ability to escape a submerged, upside-down cockpit.

No Pants Required

With my FAA Certification and instrument rating freshly issued, I was ready to tackle the Pacific crossing. The certification, made possible due to my Australian licence, meant I could fly in clouds and bad weather—skills I'd soon hone further.

I flew to the US and picked up the aircraft from Scottsdale, Arizona. A couple of test flights around the area proved interesting—Air Traffic Control seemed to find my accent endlessly amusing. Little did I know, this was just a taste of the communication challenges yet to come.

My first real test came when I was flying to Torrance, just south of LAX. Entering Los Angeles airspace, I listened intently to the other pilots, trying to get a feel for the local lingo. I was determined to nail the cadence and inflection of the American pilots.

When it was finally my turn to make the call, I mustered all my courage and spoke. Then... silence. *Had I done something wrong? Was the microphone faulty?*

'Ma'am, we don't know what you're saying,' came their confused reply.

I'm failing the radio call because of my Australian accent.

After a few attempts at speaking as clearly as possible, each word enunciated like I was teaching English to toddlers, I finally got clearance and landed at Torrance. Sitting on the tarmac, I laughed at the absurdity of not being able to communicate—despite speaking the same language. If this was a sign of things to come, I was in for an interesting journey.

Next came the task of 'tanking' the aircraft for ferry flying. This wasn't your average fill-up at the local petrol station. Small aircraft will typically fly for 5 ½ hours with a range of up to 700nm (nautical miles). My longest leg would be 13 ½ hrs (if the winds were good) and the shortest 5 hrs (again if the winds were in my favour), so I needed some serious modifications.

The solution involved removing the back seats and fitting a 750-litre rubber tank. The fuel bladder was plumbed in using a Christian pump, a hand pump, to manually transfer fuel from the bladder to the right wing.

The left-wing fuel tank would be filled to capacity prior to take off, and I would have no way of refilling it in flight, only the right wing. This meant I'd be playing a constant game of 'fuel Tetris' throughout the journey. Every 70 minutes, I would need to switch the fuel selector to the left wing, then hand-pump like my life depended on it (because it did), until the gauge read *Full* or fuel spilled out over the wing; then switch back to the right wing. This process would take about 10 minutes each time. This would be my in-flight entertainment.

Before embarking upon the Big Journey over the ocean, I did a 'proving' flight around Lake Tahoe to check the engine data. It was beautiful scenery, however I was too busy taking copious notes on the aircraft's performance to fully appreciate it. Fuel gauges, consumption rates, exhaust gas temperature—I was drowning in numbers.

After 5½ hours of flying and enough notes to write a small novel, I returned to Torrance. The fuel usage was a bit high, so the engineers replaced one of the six cylinders. A second test flight showed improved fuel consumption, but then we noticed the oil consumption was higher than expected. One step forward, two steps back.

I wouldn't be able to replenish the oil traditionally as I (naturally) wasn't prepared to step out of the plane, mid-air, and try to access the engine. I needed access from the cockpit. The engineers and I came up with an idea.

We got creative and channelled our inner 'MacGyver', this time a quote from the Merriam-Webster dictionary:

> ... *after Angus MacGyver, protagonist of the U.S. television series MacGyver (1985-92), known for regularly improvising solutions to practical problems with limited tools and materials)*

We ran a tube from the cockpit, through the firewall into the engine bay, and plumbed it into the engine oil cap. We had to figure out how to feed oil through the tube mid-flight; what was the sophisticated tool we decided for this delicate operation? A child's toy syringe! I'd be using a toy to keep my, very real, very airborne plane from running out of oil. It wasn't elegant, but it would do the job.

The firewall is an aluminium wall, between the engine and the cockpit, keeping engine noise, heat, and fumes from the cockpit. Carbon monoxide indicators in the cockpit are required, as the gas is colourless, with no odour, and is fatal for humans. I had just drilled a hole in this wall to pipe through the new oil replenishment system. I installed two carbon monoxide indicators, just to be sure.

Replenishing would require a pint of oil added to the engine for every 5 hours of flying. Considering my first leg was going to be 13 ½ hours, I would need to replenish up to 3 pints of oil over the course of the first leg of my flight. Each syringe full was just under ½ a litre, a messy business whilst flying.

Squeezing oil into the engine and pumping fuel into the wing would ensure I stayed in the air.

Another factor to consider on this long journey was something I discovered on the ferry flight I had done from New Zealand to Australia. Small planes don't have toilets. On that journey, the male pilot was able to relieve himself into a juice bottle. I had to hold my wee for over 5 hours. It was also the last time I would fly a small plane with pants on.

I'd be wearing a skirt and carrying several TravelJohns—devices filled with absorbent material that can hold a litre of liquid. Using them mid-flight would require some careful manoeuvring to avoid pushing the control column with my derriére.

With the plane modified for the long journey, and resembling a flying fuel tank, I still needed FAA approval to take off overweight. I got dispensation for up to 30% over the usual maximum, with the caveat that I couldn't bank more than 30 degrees. This meant I wasn't covered by insurance for any structural issues; I would need to be extra careful. No barrel rolls then.

I flew to Hollister, south of San Francisco, for its 6-kilometre runway. Long runways are a heavily loaded plane's best friend. There, I realised I didn't have a High Frequency (HF) radio. A trip to Radio Shack in San Francisco solved that problem, with an enthusiastic salesman (and aspiring actor) helping to install it. He was so invested in my adventure that he even came to see me off the next day! I hope he achieved his acting dreams—he certainly had a flair for the dramatic.

It's a requirement to have fuel reserves in case you need to divert or be put into a holding pattern. The legal requirement is to land with 30 minutes of diversionary or holding fuel; unless you declare an emergency. My first sector was going to be 13 ½ hours long and I would be landing with 90 minutes of fuel left, if everything went to plan.

With everything set: fuel, oil, radio, life jacket, life raft, axe (to potentially cut myself out of the aircraft), satellite phone, water, flares, emergency beacon, GPS (three of them, just in case), batteries, charts, visas, $10,000 in cash (for fuel and smoothing my way through customs), and pre-emptied cans of insecticide for customs (some countries require cabin crew to spray a whole can of insecticide throughout the cabin on landing, no matter the size of the plane. I didn't want to be emptying a whole can into my tiny cockpit on arrival, so I had pre-emptied most of the content, ready for inspection on arrival)—I was ready to go.

Mother Nature had other ideas.

It took two weeks for headwinds to die down enough to make the fuel calculations work. Two weeks of anxious waiting: checking weather reports; and constantly questioning my life choices.

Finally, the winds cooperated, and I was good to go. I started up the Beechcraft Bonanza, taxied to the runway, made my calls, and with my 750kg bladder of fuel took off out of Hollister.

Everything was going well, except my climb rate was much slower than expected—only about 200ft per minute instead of 500–1000ft. It was like trying to climb stairs while carrying a hippopotamus. Two hours in, I hit a snag. I was in and out of different airspace, and requesting clearance each time, however there was one clearance I needed to enter into US oceanic airspace, and they needed to test that my HF radio was working. I switched to the required frequency, keeping the VHF frequency open as well, and made the call, but it didn't work.

The radio that we'd just installed. The radio that was supposed to be my lifeline across the Pacific. *That* radio.

I had been flying for 2 hours and couldn't turn back because I was too heavy to land.

Time is fuel and money. I was committed. I decided to keep going.

I repeated my radio call. Still nothing. On VHF they said to me, 'Have you made your call?'

'Yes, and I heard you,' I lied. I didn't want to turn back. I thought I could just bullshit my way out of this.

'We didn't hear you. Please repeat your call.'

I was stalling as much as I could, getting further and further out to sea. I managed to stall them for about an hour, now 3 hours into my flight.

'Ma'am, you're going to have to turn around, because we require you to have a working HF radio.'

'No, no, I'm good. I've got a satellite phone. I'm ok. I'll accept this,' I replied.

'No, you have to turn back.'

I tried to refuse again.

After more stalling, I was given an ultimatum: turn back or be shot down by military jets.

Whether they would have followed through or not, I didn't want to find out. I turned around, taking 2½ hours to return to Hollister, then another hour circling to burn off fuel before landing. It was a long, frustrating journey to end up right back where I started.

Landing overweight was tricky. I used the entire 6km runway, keeping my speed up and doing a slow turn with brake against power to avoid tipping the Bonanza on its tail. The engineers met me with a 44-gallon drum and a tyre to support the tail as I shut down. It was like a pit stop, but instead of changing tyres, we were trying to keep the plane from doing a wheelie.

We discovered a loose wire on the antenna was the culprit for the radio issues. Once fixed, I tried to get some sleep before my second attempt. Unfortunately, sleep eluded me that night. My mind was too busy running through various worst-case scenarios *and* questioning my sanity.

After a horrible night of tossing and turning, I checked the winds. Still favourable. I went to the airport early, and took off for my second attempt at a flight across the Pacific from the USA to Australia.

This time, I got through the airspace checks. The controllers seemed relieved to see me go, probably hoping they wouldn't have to deal with me again. I couldn't blame them—I was a handful.

The first leg was 13 ½ hours from Hollister to Hilo, Hawaii.

It was a constant juggling act of switching between fuel tanks, pumping fuel, and adding oil. It was a race against time because if the left wing ran out of fuel, so did I. Hopefully I had calculated enough reserves and head wind.

When not occupied with keeping the plane in the air, I kept a flight log, read books, drew, and made pictures out of the clouds. Anything to keep my mind active and avoid the creeping dread of being alone over a vast ocean in a tiny plane.

I was constantly listening out for any engine upset or splutter.

One of the more interesting aspects of the journey was chatting on the pilot's frequency 123.45. These conversations provided some much-needed entertainment:

'Aircraft 6,500 feet, west of Monterey, do you read?'

'November 3576 Lima is 300 nautical miles west off Monterey. Maintaining 6,500. Go ahead.'

'November 3576 Lima go numbers.'

'November 3576 Lima, on numbers.'

"What the hell are you flying?" they asked.

I told them.

'Where are you from?' they asked.

I told them.

'Where are you going?' they asked.

I told them.

'Are you fucking crazy?!'

This happened a few times with commercial airlines overhead. It was amusing and helped relieve the pressure, even if it did draw attention to my rather tenuous situation. Other pilots since have called me bonkers, mad, insane, crazy, and only occasionally 'big balls'. I did question the wisdom of my decision to fly this journey, but I was too far in to back out now.

As my fuel burned, I navigated low cloud, rain, and strong winds, but finally I was approaching land.

As I approached Hilo, I was exhausted. My legs were numb, my brain foggy, and I was dehydrated, unfamiliar with the airspace, and in full cloud. It was like trying to land a plane while drunk and blindfolded. Luckily, the controllers heard my accent and guided me in safely. Their patience with my sleep-deprived attempts at communication was admirable.

Stepping onto solid ground was a *huge* relief. I could barely walk when I stepped out of the aircraft, but I was glad my feet were feeling land under them. The first leg was over, but the journey was far from finished.

Kiribati was the next leg. Then Faleolo, Norfolk Island, Lord Howe Island, and finally Australia.

I'd been told that if you had to ditch, it is best to do it in US waters. Their coast guard could rescue you within 8–10 hours. Heading into international waters, I wasn't as confident about timely rescue. It was a sobering thought as I prepared for the next leg.

Landing into Kiribati was an experience. No fencing around the airport and red crabs everywhere. It was like landing on a different planet. The anticipation built as I approached the atoll in the middle of the Pacific Ocean, near where Amelia Earhart was rumoured to have disappeared on her last flight. Despite having GPS navigation equipment, I also relied on the island's NDB, which they manually activated for scheduled arrivals. Following protocol, I conducted a precautionary overfly to assess the runway conditions, wind direction, and potential obstacles. The crabs scattered across the runway were certainly unique, yet it was safe to land.

The local community were extremely friendly, handling paperwork with genuine warmth and smiles. The eleven-hour flight from Hilo had been considerably shorter than the previous day, though still demanding. I'd chosen to fly only during daylight hours for safety and peace of mind, particularly if ocean ditching became necessary.

My next planned destination was Faleolo, Samoa. However, several hours into the seven hour flight, an HF radio call informed me they lacked the fuel I'd ordered. Poring over my charts, I recalculated fuel and endurance figures, determining I could divert to Pago Pago, merely 25 nautical miles from my original destination. Given the islands' limited fuel supplies, delivered by ship, I made a satellite phone call to secure my order—at a significantly inflated price. Upon landing, the price increased further until we negotiated a cash payment in USD.

Though exhaustion suggested an extra day's rest, approaching inclement weather forced me to stick with the planned departure. The next leg to Norfolk Island took eight hours against strong headwinds. As with my flight from New Zealand, I flew between 500-1000 feet above the ocean to minimise their impact.

Australian quarantine procedures proved amusing. The local police officer, wearing multiple hats including border control, demonstrated practical wisdom regarding the insecticide requirements. Through an unspoken understanding, the official process was creatively satisfied, aided by a box of chocolates.

A rough engine cylinder prompted me to seek assistance. Fortunately, a mainland Australian engineer resided on Norfolk Island, equipped with essential tools and some parts. His makeshift repair would suffice until reaching the mainland. The forced pause allowed for some welcome island exploration.

Two days later, I departed for Lord Howe Island, merely three hours away. The final stretch included a quick refuel, a pre-ordered hamburger, customs clearance, then two hours to Kempsey. I audibly sighed with relief upon hearing Australian Air Traffic Control. I had made it. Soon I would see my son, though my commercial licence hours remained slightly incomplete.

The following day, after removing the ferry tank and oil system and reinstalling rear seats, I delivered the aircraft to its Victorian owner.

Years later, when I met the love of my life (he wrote that sentence), he bragged he was born in Kiribati. I trumped him by saying I had landed there in a Beechcraft Bonanza. Not many people can say that.

In further decisions that would make most people question my sanity, I did that trip again—two more times. Each trip was as challenging as the first, with its own unique obstacles and moments of terror. However, each successful crossing built my confidence and skills.

Other pilots typically choose to fly the safer (but much longer, and predominantly over land) routes, back to Australia. Think Alaska, Russia, Japan, Taiwan, Philippines, Indonesia, Darwin onwards.

These three ferry flights earned me enough hours, but also many transferable skills I would carry forward: Resourcefulness, innovation, and even international relations. The $10K USD came in handy, especially when fuel prices mysteriously doubled on one island.

It was a stark reminder that when it is the only fuel in town, you don't have much bargaining power.

I didn't get paid to fly these 'insane' over-water trips, but I had my hours, and a story that makes most pilots' jaws drop. Not bad for a girl who once couldn't even keep her breakfast down during a simple flight!

Looking back, I realise how much these journeys shaped me as a pilot *and* as a person. The challenges I faced—from communication difficulties to mechanical issues, from fuel management to battling fatigue—all contributed to making me a more competent and confident aviator.

The Pacific crossings taught me the true meaning of self-reliance. When you're alone in a small plane over vast expanses of ocean, there's absolutely no one to turn to but yourself. Every decision, every calculation, every adjustment could mean the difference between success and disaster. It was a responsibility that weighed heavily on me but also empowered me.

I learned to trust my instincts and my training, to stay calm in the face of adversity, and to problem-solve on the fly (quite literally). The creative solutions we came up with—like the toy syringe for oil replenishment—showed me that with enough ingenuity, almost *any* problem can be solved.

These experiences also gave me a deep appreciation for the vastness and beauty of our planet. Flying for hours over endless blue, watching the sun rise and set from above the clouds, seeing remote islands appear on the horizon like tiny oases in a vast desert—these are sights that few people get to experience, and I feel incredibly privileged to have done so.

There were also many moments of fear, doubt, and sheer exhaustion, times when I questioned my decision to undertake such a risky endeavour. Pushing through those moments, facing my fears and overcoming them, a wonderful sense of accomplishment bloomed inside me.

As I reflect on these journeys, I'm struck by how they mirror life itself. There are moments of beauty and wonder, interspersed with periods of challenge and fear. There are unexpected obstacles to overcome, decisions to be made with only limited information, and long stretches where perseverance is the only option. And like life itself, the journey is more important than the destination.

These Pacific crossings were a serious test of my character, a journey of self-discovery, and they fulfilled my need for adventure. They taught me that with enough determination, preparation, and a dash of craziness, even the most daunting challenges can be overcome.

Lady MacGyver

It was during those long stretches between islands over the Pacific that I began to recognise a pattern in my life, a coping mechanism that had been with me since childhood: my alter ego. This other version of myself had been my silent partner through every challenge, every new beginning; and now, every ocean crossing.

As an RAAF brat (child of someone in the Airforce), I was no stranger to change. We moved schools many times, a prospect that would have been scary and off-putting if it weren't for my parents' sage advice: 'See it as an adventure, Michelle.'

Little did they know, they were helping me reprogram my relationship with change and fear.

Before each house move, I'd immerse myself in research about the new school and town. I'd study maps, any local attractions, swimming locations, tennis, dancing, or anything I was interested in at the time. This preparation gave me a sense of control and also things to look forward to, transforming fear into excitement.

I wasn't turning up to these new schools as the scared little girl; instead, I stepped into the shoes of my alter ego—a confident, smiling version of myself. She didn't have a name yet, but she was confident.

I was tall and skinny, often sporting a bowl cut; nerdy and into sport. I didn't fit into any box, but my alter ego's constant smile and head-on approach to challenges masked the nervous little girl within.

Wonder Woman on the TV had made quite an impact on me. I think part of my alter ego was channelling her confidence and poise.

Even though I was shy and insecure inside, the persona I projected at school inspired my teachers to elect me school Captain. I even received public speaking awards whilst safely ensconced within my alter ego's skin.

This pattern continued into my flying career. Remember that first flying lesson where I showed up in full uniform? Classic alter ego move. She might have thrown up, but she got me airborne.

Over time, I began to recognise the switch that triggered my alter ego: butterflies in the stomach and the urge to visit the bathroom. This physical response became my cue to step into my other self, my *braver* self.

As I sat in the cockpit, holding a toy syringe and pumping fuel into the wing, I realized there was more to my alter ego than just Wonder Woman's poise. There was a touch of MacGyver in there too. When faced with a barrier, I always found a way around it, just like MacGyver, with his improvisational problem-solving.

This MacGyver-esque thinking had been with me since high school and then continued into university. I'd chosen 3 Unit Textiles, 3 Unit Art, and Photography—all expensive subjects. To make it work, I was constantly scavenging things from the roadside to repurpose into artwork. Most of my uni art used 'found objects', a testament to my ability to create solutions from whatever was at hand.

It was there, flying over the Pacific, that I finally gave my alter ego a name: Lady MacGyver. She was the perfect blend of Wonder

Woman's poise and MacGyver's ingenuity. Lady MacGyver has allowed me to forge ahead when fear wanted to hold me back.

I have since learned that many successful people don alter egos to help them be their best. Beyoncé becomes Sasha Fierce; Kobe Bryant transformed into the Black Mamba, and David Bowie was Ziggy Stardust. We *all* have the capacity to be more than we think we are, to step into a version of ourselves that can handle whatever challenges come our way.

Who is your alter ego?

Lady MacGyver

Miss Identify

Lady MacGyver was my alter ego but 'Miss Identify' became my nickname for a short time, bestowed upon me by Oliver, who was instructing me for my commercial licence.

I was training for my first twin-engine endorsement. Oliver instructed me through the usual effects of control, climbing, descending, and turning.

You'd think single and twin-engine are similar, but they aren't. There's an old saying:

> *If the engine fails in a single engine aircraft, you glide to the place of landing; if an engine fails in a twin-engine aircraft, the good engine simply takes you to the scene of the crash.*

We had finished our manoeuvres and were coming back in.

'Turn on the landing lights,' instructed Oliver.

I reached down and accidentally turned off the left engine magnetos. The magnetos provide ignition to the engine, and I had just turned off half our propulsion.

The immediate yaw turned (swung) the nose of the aircraft to the dead engine side. Oliver was straight onto it, executing a textbook failed engine recovery, not realising it was student-pilot-induced. *I* had done it.

He looked over at the controls to my side, then looked at me and said, 'What the fuck? You turned off the magnetos!' He calmed quickly. 'Ok, we'll start again.'

We continued to the inbound reporting point for Bankstown airport.

'Ok. Turn on the landing lights,' he repeated.

I turned off the left engine magnetos again!

FUUUCK!

It's no excuse, but the Piper Seneca II really should have a cover or guard over critical switches to make it *difficult* to accidentally turn them off.

Oliver again repeated the textbook engine recovery and pronounced my new nickname.

'I'm going to call you Miss Identify from now on!'

Luckily, I didn't give him any further reason to repeat the nickname, and I became hyper-vigilant about which switch is which. It was a humbling reminder that even experienced pilots can make mistakes, and that attention to detail is *crucial* in aviation.

Testing Times

Remember when I said Lady MacGyver liked a challenge? Well, she outdid herself this time. To get my Commercial licence I did something unprecedented in Australia. The regulators even challenged it, but duly found that all conditions were legal, all requirements were met, and therefore I was legitimate.

I had built up my hours with the ferry flying and other trips, and was ready to do my Commercial flight test. My testing officer, Les Morris, was known at the airport for pushing the envelope in his chase for the dollar. After running it by the chief flying instructor, he asked if I would be interested in combining the different flight tests together and roll them all into one big flight. I was keen—the faster I got qualified, the sooner I would get paid to fly.

Les was a character with a fascinating past. He had real life experiences flying both fixed wing aircraft and, earlier on, helicopters in the Vietnam war. He is quite famous for the photographs he took of soldiers running to his chopper, with absolute fear and hope in their eyes, which can be seen at the Australian War Memorial.

Les knew the rules extremely well, always pushing up close to them, never *breaking* them, however doing things differently enough to put some pilots off. I wanted my commercial licence, so was happy to accept his plan.

The morning started with a pre-flight briefing of how the day was to unfold. I was to be 'Captain' for the day and was to treat the flight as such. Les told me about the scenarios where I would be 'Visual,' or under

'Instrument' conditions, and what was expected of me. Not only would I fly within the tolerance required of the Civil Aviation Safety Authority (CASA), but I would also meet all the requirements of a Captain that related to passenger comfort, including all safety briefings that would be required during our flight.

Knowing this, I had prepared catering including tea and coffee, water, biscuits, sandwiches and lollies. I included wipes, napkins, a sick bag (just in case), and a selection of magazines. I'd even created an in-seat pocket safety card for my pretend charter company. Again, *the most pilot-y pilot who ever piloted* remember?

We took off from Bankstown Airport in the Piper Seneca II, a small twin engine 6-seater often used for training because it was basic. The longest series of tests had begun in my 11 hour marathon.

I had the 'hood' on for take-off, an IFR view-limiting visor, which when worn, prevented view out the front window, limiting vision to the aircraft instruments only, ensuring I couldn't see outside and had to rely solely on the instruments. We flew this first sector, departing a GAAP aerodrome (General Aviation Aerodrome Procedures), under Instrument Flight Rules (IFR), to Nowra, to conduct an ILS (Instrument Landing System).

Commencing the approach, both engines were functioning, with one engine's power being reduced to simulate a failed engine, just before intercepting the localiser glide path. Having trained for this, it went smoothly and as expected. After successfully conducting the approach, and being told 'not visual,' I conducted a single-engine 'Missed Approach' (baulked approach where all available power is used to 'take-off' again and climb to a safe altitude to either try again, or consider your options.)

We left the military airbase in Nowra under Visual Flight Rules (VFR). From Nowra we flew to Canberra visually (using the terrain to navigate:

highways, railway lines, power lines and Lake Bathurst as the inbound reporting point). Canberra is also a military airbase, (which was a Class D airspace at the time, now a Class C airspace. Australia's civil airspace system mirrors that of the USA, with different categories from Class A to Class G)

In Canberra, we conducted a touch and go and then landed to refuel. I took this opportunity for a comfort break and to get my head ready for the next part of the test. Les wasn't giving me any hint as to how I was going with the tests, ,which I took as a positive sign.

After departing Canberra, we dropped to 300ft and contour-flew around Yass, being mindful of the powerlines and hilly terrain and valleys. I was given the task of finding a particular dirt road, with an imaginary cloud ceiling of 600ft. Everything goes fast at that altitude, so slowing down was key.

I located the dirt road and flew along it; Les, in the meantime, had rung his wife and instructed her to open two paddock gates on their property. My task was to muster his 80 head of cattle through one gate, into the first paddock, and then muster them into the *next* paddock. It took a couple of goes as the cows were not happy, nor compliant.

I didn't expect cattle herding to be part of my test!

After successfully getting all the cows into the same paddock, we flew to Goulburn. It was getting close to the end of the day component of the test, so we ate the sandwiches I'd made and waited for last light.

We departed Goulburn under the Night Visual Flight Rules and flew 3 circuits. We then flew visually to Bindook, which is an IFR reporting point, over the ranges. The Piper Seneca II is not known for its power, so it took a long time to climb to 10,000ft. We then overlaid the Mudgee VOR (short-range radio) instrument approach. This was a bit dodgy. The Flight Plan was approved, so legal, but we were pretending to do an instrument approach over an inbound reporting point, that RPT (Regular Public Transport Aircraft) were using as an approach point into Bankstown or Sydney. We weren't landing from this approach, so implemented a fake 'ceiling' set to zero. We then flew Night VFR back to Bankstown.

All up it was 6½ hours of flying over an 11-hour day. I was completely exhausted when we finished, but at the end of this marathon test, I was a commercially licenced pilot with:

- A command instrument rating
- A private IFR rating
- A night VFR rating
- Low level flying endorsement, and
- A mustering endorsement

Les charged full price for each test, but I didn't mind. I could *finally* be paid to fly.

The next day, without pause for celebration, I started my instructor rating. Why stop when you're on a roll?

If you are ever stuck at a party talking to a pilot (and they *will* regale you with their aeronautical adventures) and for all those non-aerosexuals out there, I recommend you read the Glossary of Terms at the front of this book.

As some wise old pilot once said, 'Any landing you can walk away from is a good landing. Any landing you can use the aircraft again is a great landing.'

By that measure, this 11-hour odyssey was definitely a *great* landing in my career as a pilot.

Lady MacGyver

Woman's First Flight

In the early 1900s, the term 'aviatrix' was used to denote a female pilot. More recently, the term has taken on a condescending tone.

When someone asks me what you call a female pilot, I resist the urge to roll my eyes and I simply respond, 'Captain,' because let's face it, the sky, and the aircraft, do not care what's between your legs when you're cruising at 30,000 feet.

In 1903, the Wright brothers managed to keep an aircraft airborne for a whopping 12 seconds. There is some conjecture that they were the first to be airborne, but one thing is for sure—women were never allowed to fly planes during those times.

Women were often considered the 'workhorses', relegated to taxiing the aircraft from hanger to hanger, or out to the airfield where the 'highly skilled' male pilot would be allowed to fly and take the glory.

Here's where it gets interesting. A favourite story of mine is about one Blanche Scott. In 1910, Blanche was taxiing an aircraft to the field and mysteriously became airborne. Her instructor, Glenn Curtiss, had fitted a limiter on the throttle to prevent her from gaining enough speed to become airborne. Rumour has it that (potentially) a gust of wind lifted the plane, but I prefer to think she moved the limiter and flew the biplane up to 40ft before executing a perfect landing. That's my kind of gal.

Amelia Earhart is another personal hero of mine. Her 1937 attempt to circumnavigate the globe ended in disaster, but she left her mark. I've flown solo over the area where she was rumoured to have crashed. It was my own little tribute to a woman who dared to soar when others said she should stay grounded.

Humans have been enamoured of flight for a very long time.

Abbas ibn Firnas, a 9th-century polymath, decided to play bird for a day. He covered himself in feathers, strapped on some silk and wood wings, and took a leap of faith. Witnesses say he flew a considerable distance before gravity reminded him it was still in charge. He hurt his back on landing, which is why I prefer my flights with a bit more horsepower and a lot less feathers.

Looking back at these 20th century female pioneers, I can't help but feel a mix of awe and frustration. Awe at their courage and ingenuity, and frustration at the barriers they faced. But mostly, I feel grateful. Grateful that their perseverance paved the way for pilots like me to take to the skies without having to ruffle too many feathers (unless we want to, of course).

The next time someone calls me an 'aviatrix', I'll continue to smile politely and correct them. It's not about being a female pilot or a male pilot. It's about being a damn good pilot, full stop.

'The most difficult thing is the decision to act, the rest is merely tenacity." - Amelia Earhart

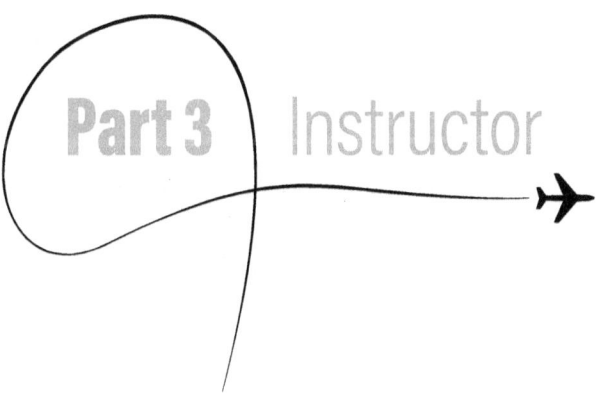

Part 3 Instructor

*'Aviation is proof that given the will,
we have the capacity to achieve the impossible.' -
Eddie Rickenbacker*

After passing my Commercial Pilot Licence check, I could now officially be paid to fly. The only problem was that I didn't have the mandatory experience (hours) to satisfy company or insurance requirements.

The aviation industry sets strict minimums for pilot hours, creating the familiar challenge for new commercial pilots: you need hours to get hired, but you need to be hired to gain hours. The options for gaining these hours were limited, but clear.

I could pay for a cadetship with an airline, retraining over 12–18 months at significant personal expense. There was the traditional path of flying 'up north' to remote islands, which wasn't feasible as a single mum with a by now three-year-old child. Parachute operations offered excellent take-off and landing practice but didn't align with my career goals.

Flight instruction emerged as the practical choice. I could stay in Sydney, maintain regular hours for my child, and develop deeper aviation expertise through teaching others. The decision wasn't only about building the necessary hours, it was about finding the right path that balanced professional growth with my family responsibilities.

Take off Power

Flying is about precision. It's also about praying your student doesn't accidentally kill you both.

We were in a Piper Cherokee at the holding point of the runway, waiting for clearance to enter and take-off. My student was rehearsing what he'd say to the control tower on the radio. We received clearance and lined up on the piano keys (pilot-speak for the white stripes at the end of the runway), applied full power and started hurtling down the runway. I'm pretty sure my student stopped breathing around that point. The aircraft then became airborne. We were flying!

I was teaching him how to fly a circuit. A circuit is a flight pattern, basically a rectangle with five 'legs', so named to describe the flight phase you are in with rules around when you can join or leave the circuit. This assists in planning and building a picture of where other traffic may be when hearing and giving radio calls. The legs of the circuit are Upwind, X-Wind, Downwind, Base and Final. A part of the circuit training would include a 'Touch and Go' procedure, another term for practicing take-offs and landings in a continual flow, with only a brief 'touch' on the runway.

We were flying upwind, climbing away from the runway. He was a great student and had been rehearsing his patter (self-talk), what he needs to do and when, almost like a script, and he'd started brilliantly.

'Hand on throttle, maintain centreline allowing for drift, nose up slowly to 5 degrees, breathe'. I always added 'breathe' to any instruction, as one can often forget. He continued, 'At 500ft turn 30 degrees Angle of Bank to turn onto a heading of 200 degrees'. This was perfect, except we were already approaching 800ft and close to an International Airport's control area—a mistake which could put us in the news for all the wrong reasons.

I helped steer the aircraft onto a heading 90-ish degrees from our current heading and gently, but firmly, pushed the control column forward, forcing the nose down, stopping the rapid climb into overhead traffic.

My student was visibly sweating, so I helped him with the manual handling component whilst he continued the flight sequence. We turned downwind and ran through the pre-landing checks: BUMFISH (there's an acronym for everything in aviation, and no, it's not a weird sea creature). Brakes – off; Undercarriage – down (or fixed and welded in this case); Mixture – full rich; Fuel – on (and enough); Instruments and Indications – normal; Switches – on (magnetos, lights etc), and Hatches and Harnesses – secure... and breathe.

Like patting your head and rubbing your tummy, these checks need to be completed whilst talking on the radio, steering the aircraft, controlling the power, extending landing flaps and making a descending turn. My student was doing all these while trying not to pass out. Multi-tasking at its finest.

Base turn came up quickly and then the turn on to final approach. Cue the 'Top Gun' theme in my head. (Am I the only one?) Those familiar with the movie, 'Top Gun' will understand the silent request most aerosexuals have in their mind when coming in to land— 'Tower, this is Ghost Rider requesting a flyby.' Air Boss Johnson replies, 'Negative, Ghost Rider, the pattern is full.'

My student was sweating profusely now, and his eyes could not open any wider. I pull him back to the task of landing the aircraft, and doing his first touch and go. Speed is good, altitude is great, and the aiming point is perfect. Bang, we're on.

We had completed the 'touch' component, and needed to get a wriggle on for the 'go' part before we ran out of runway.

I'm sure he had lost the power of speech *and* thought; his eyes had continued to grow wide like saucers at the rapidly approaching end of the runway.

I reset the aircraft flaps, trimmed the nose and called, 'Set take-off power,' possibly with a *little* more urgency than I would have liked to.

The funny thing about stress, it effects your hearing. He heard "Take-off Power". He then proceeded to Take. Off. The. Power. My turn to sweat now.

We were slowing, although still too fast to stop, yet not fast enough to take-off again. Every expletive raced through my mind and for the sake of my student (and my professional reputation), I kept them all inside.

My training kicked in. I adjusted the flaps, slammed on full power, and we were airborne again. I'm not sure if we touched the grass at the end of the runway, but it was close. We then bugged out of the circuit and flew around long enough for me to extract the seat cushion from between my buttocks; and breathe.

We landed and debriefed the lesson, including the huge learning *I* had.

Turns out, my student couldn't recall a single word I'd said in the aircraft. Stress, noise, fear, and a new environment had turned my clear instructions into pure gibberish. It was a stark reminder that in aviation, miscommunication can be fatal.

We train hard to make sure mistakes don't happen.

The good news? That sweaty, terrified student is now an Airline Captain for Emirates and a great friend. I like to think I played a small part in that success. This experience reinforced the importance of staying calm under pressure and communicating clearly. As an instructor, your students look to you for guidance and reassurance. If you panic, *they* panic.

The next time you're on a flight and hear the Captain's voice, remember this: behind that calm exterior is someone who's probably had their fair share of *Holy crap!* moments. It's all part of the journey from nerve-wracked student to cool, collected Captain.

Lady MacGyver

Lost 3,000 Feet Doing a Wee

Kym was an entrepreneurial businesswoman who had built a successful financial payments company. She also owned a brand-new, single engine, 4-seater Trinidad.

As I instructed her to fly said plane, we became good friends. Thankfully, Kym also had an adventurous spirit and wasn't content with boring old navigation exercises around Bankstown airport. We mixed it up and flew around Australia.

Why practice landings when you can have an adventure?

Being an accomplished equestrian, Kym suggested we fly to Birdsville for a navigation exercise, then combine it with a cattle muster on horseback to Marree. We'd get a helicopter ride back to Birdsville and fly back to Sydney. As an instructor, this sounded much more entertaining than watching students bounce off the runway for the umpteenth time, plus, I'd never visited that part of the country.

Her aircraft was beautiful, fully kitted out with all the bells and whistles. Dual GPS, all the latest technology, and a full glass cockpit, something not usually attainable in private aircraft.

Every flight, I taught something that would help the pilot in an emergency. On the way to Birdsville, I covered her instruments with big paper charts (Maps), the type we use to navigate *without* GPS.

'If I lose the GPS, I'll just land,' Kym said, with all the confidence of someone who's never been lost in the Outback.

I responded, 'In an ideal world, yes, but in the middle of the desert, or over a city, you can't practically do that.'

To drive the point home, I pulled the throttle back to idle and challenged her to land. One look out the window at the vast nothingness below, and she got the message, loud and clear.

I told her that when using these charts you need to be able to determine where you are at *any* given time. It's also a requirement to get your licence.

The charts we use are so good that out in the Strzelecki Desert you can actually point out the different ranges, culverts and rivulets on the terrain. We use triangulation to be 100% confident of our location and take a heading from that.

We had all the charts out covering the screens so she could find her location without the instrumentation. We were in the middle of the desert, flying at 6,500 feet, when she announced she needed to do a wee.

As previously mentioned, my experiences of the long flights, island hopping in small aircraft, from the USA back to Australia, taught me the importance of always carrying a TravelJohn. This is a device used by both males and females for when nature calls and there's no bathroom in sight. A bag filled with absorbent beads with a contoured opening that holds approximately a litre of fluid which it instantly turns into a thick, disposable gel. A fancy porta-potty.

I offered her a TravelJohn, to which she responded, 'What the hell is that!'

We were very good friends, but not THAT close, so we proceeded to erect a Great Wall of Charts between us for privacy, whilst she attempted her first TravelJohn experience. I was well versed in their use; Kym was about to discover that there is a technique, and hers wasn't the right one.

We had the autopilot on. Kym managed to turn herself around, kneeling on her seat, facing the back of the plane, TravelJohn in hand. As we all do in uncomfortable positions, she developed stage fright and couldn't pee.

The mixture of discomfort and awkwardness made her start to laugh. I started to laugh. And then I noticed we were descending slightly.

'Get your arse off the control column!' I shouted, which only made us laugh harder. I looked out the window to offer her more privacy; while silently praying she hadn't eaten any asparagus. Yep, kinda gross.

She finally got in the flow. Not wanting to break her concentration, I continued to look out the window, desperately trying to stifle my laughter.

Here's the thing about weeing: once you start, it's very hard to stop. Now Kym was worrying that she had two litres attempting to enter a vessel that only held one!

Our uncontrolled laughter took our attention away from the fact that we had descended 3,000 feet and had completely missed the autopilot alarms that sound when you deviate by over 300 feet in altitude. Kym's derriere was trying to land the plane.

Fortunately, there was only one litre, otherwise, the outcome might have been very different.

That trip took us from Sydney, to Dubbo, on to Bourke and then Birdsville. We parked the plane and met up with a group for the cattle muster.

Kym was an accomplished rider; she had once been a jockey. A professional. When we were getting paired with our horses, she claimed that she was only 'competent'. This was a great lesson. Other people, who bragged about their expertise, were partnered with horses that weren't as well behaved as others.

Kym thoughtfully decided on a slower horse so we could ride together at my decidedly amateur pace. Our brumbies were gentle souls.

For seven days, we ambled along with a diverse group, droving cattle through the Outback. At night, we 'glamped' in comfort that would make five-star hotels jealous. Picture doonas, white towels, showers, and hair dryers. Chef-cooked meals with wine around a *huge* campfire. Not exactly the *rugged* Outback experience, but hey, I wasn't complaining.

The track we rode was from Birdsville to Marree, a very dry and dusty route. A couple of horses forgot they had riders and decided to scratch an itch by rolling in the sand. Those riders got an express trip to Adelaide courtesy of the Royal Flying Doctor Service.

Dick Smith, the famous Australian entrepreneur, flew in for a couple of days, and regaled us with his aviation experiences. We didn't let on that we had flown there ourselves. (Sometimes it's better to listen than to engage in aerial one-upmanship.)

We also met two friendly New Zealanders (Kiwis) who invited us on a horse-riding wine tour of Hawkes Bay. We took them up on that offer, which is where I discovered that after visiting two wineries on horseback, I developed the confidence of The Man from Snowy River. A few wines under my belt, and I started to believe I'd bounce if I fell. Spoiler alert: humans don't bounce.

I didn't charge Kym for all the lessons; instead, she generously paid for all our experiences. She was an amazing friend. Sadly, she later suffered an injury while working on her property and didn't recover. I think about her often, remembering our adventures and her infectious laughter.

We may have lost 3000 feet doing a wee and laughed about it afterward, but the lesson stuck with me. Tiny distractions matter, especially in flying. An aircraft just one degree off course at the start can end up miles from its intended destination within an hour. In flying, as in life, small mistakes quickly become big problems. Regular check-ins and staying focused keep you safely on track.

—Blue skies and tail winds, Kym xx

Following the Magenta Line

Early in my flying career, every airborne hour was crucial. Airlines want pilots with *extensive* experience, so I was always looking for ways to build up my flight time.

Patrick Watson, the Chief Pilot at the flying school I worked in, was one of my first mentors. He gave me some powerful life-changing advice:

'It's up to you whether you fly one hour a thousand times, or one thousand individual hours'. In other words, don't just follow the magenta line.

For non-pilots, 'following the magenta line' means mindlessly following the GPS track, a pink line on the screen. That pink line can be dangerously misleading. GPS outages, system failures, data entry errors, or even accidentally hitting 'Execute' instead of 'Delete' when modifying the flight plan, can make that magenta line unreliable.

There's a famous lecture called 'Children of the Magenta Line' that went viral in aviation circles. It highlights how pilots (and people in general) were becoming overly reliant on automation, mindlessly following a path rather than thinking for themselves. It's a wake-up call that resonates way beyond the cockpit.

Patrick's advice echoed this sentiment: Don't be the pilot who flies the same route a thousand times on autopilot, eyes glued to that deceptive pink line. Instead, make each flight a *new* learning experience. Test yourself; keep your mind active and engaged.

I took that advice to heart, applying it not just to flying, but to my life. There's no point in mindlessly repeating the same routine when you could be learning something new. It's the difference between stagnation and growth.

This advice later saved me when my plane was hit by lightning (more on that later). Instead of just following the same old route, I'd made a habit of noticing everything: the topography; control steps; required descent rates; and radio frequencies. I created mnemonics and acronyms to remember all the details.

When radios and instruments fail, and they may; pilots can *only* rely on their experience. The wider and more diverse the experience; the more 'tools' they have in their kit.

Life, like flying, isn't always comfortable. But I've learned that discomfort is where growth happens. It's where you discover what you're *really* capable of.

Whether you're in a cockpit or just navigating your life: Don't be a child of the magenta line. Take the *challenging* route. Ask questions. Learn something new. Because when life's instruments fail and radios go quiet, it's your depth of experience that will save you.

Adventure and learning are a lot more exciting than flying the same hour a thousand times.

Grade 2 Dickhead

As a full-time Grade 3 instructor at a flying school, I thought I'd seen it all. Then came the day a more senior Grade 2 instructor asked me to be his 'pretend student'. He needed to practice his 'patter' and instruction technique for an upcoming renewal test.

I was always interested in how other instructors conducted their lessons, so agreed to be his pretend student.

We took off, him in the instructor's seat on the right, me flying on the left.

Everything was going smoothly until we were doing the inbound report at 2RN, approaching Bankstown Airport. I was mid-sentence on the radio when suddenly, the instructor reached over and grabbed my crotch.

My reaction was instant. I lifted my right arm, bent my elbow, and smashed it into his nose. Hard.

Through his swearing, I calmly finished my inbound radio call. Professional to the core.

'Why the fuck did you do that?' he had the audacity to ask.

Grade 2 Level Dickhead. How could you not know the answer to that question?

'Do not touch me again,' I firmly stated.

The original lesson plan was that we would be doing circuits. Touch and go, so he could practise his instructions. I changed the inbound call to a full stop landing.

He protested, but I was having none of it. We landed, I reported the incident and was assured I'd never fly with him again. *Good riddance*, I thought.

Fast-forward 18 months. The universe put Grade 2 Dickhead back into my flight path. He owned a Cessna 340 that was chartered for a flight to Hamilton Island. I was to fly the charter, but first, I needed to do a few circuits with him, for 'insurance purposes'.

We took off, the silence between us palpable. We were flying downwind and I noticed the trim was acting up. It was hard to trim forward; he was laughing throughout my attempts.

'What's wrong with the aircraft?' I asked. 'It's not trimming correctly.'

He responded with a laugh that made my skin crawl. 'I turned the trim switch around so that it's upside down. If anyone tries to steal my aircraft, they will kill themselves after trimming the wrong way and crash.'

I landed and refused to fly his death trap. The charter company, thankfully, paid for an engineer to correct the trim, and I flew to Hamilton Island safely.

Not all idiots are on the ground, some do fly planes. If and when you meet one, don't be afraid to land the plane and walk away. In aviation, as in life, *trust your instincts*. If someone tries to mess with your controls—be it your aircraft or your personal space—don't hesitate to show them the emergency exit.

Four Private Pilots Lost

I bought my first aircraft while still learning to fly. It was a Cessna 172n, a small, four-seater, single engine aircraft that cost me $22,000. It wasn't exactly state-of-the-art, but the engine was sound, and it did its job.

I used it to build up hours, visiting friends in the country or taking mum to lunch in Canberra. I also rented it out at a flying school to help cover costs; I essentially got to fly my plane for nothing—a very good investment.

While instructing at a different flying school, an elderly gentleman came in to do his Biannual Flight Review (BFR). Every two years, pilots are required to prove they are still competent and safe.

I took him up for his BFR where he mentioned that he hadn't flown very often lately, only about 8 hours in the past two years.

During our flight, it became clear he was rustier than he alluded to. He forgot crucial procedures, and I wasn't confident signing him off.

I suggested we treat this flight as a training flight and book in another session later. He didn't like that idea and went to another flying school. I wasn't offended; just hopeful he'd at least learned *something* from our session. The other school signed him off with an updated BFR.

Later, I discovered he'd hired my plane from that other flying school, and with three other pilots headed to an open day at Wedderburn Airport, southwest of Sydney.

Wedderburn Airport is tricky. It's only partially paved and surrounded by tall gum trees, which means the wind at ground level can be deceptive.

You need to know the wind direction above the trees for a safe take-off. The airport is primarily used by recreational pilots, and there is an Aeroclub.

Aircraft take off into wind; Aircraft don't go very well taking off with the wind behind them. Airflow over the wing helps to generate lift.

After the open day, the elderly pilot and his friends took off. As they reached treetop height, they hit trouble. They'd misjudged the wind direction above the trees and weren't climbing. I can only imagine their panic as those treetops loomed closer.

The pilot pulled back, trying to climb. With a tailwind, increasing your angle of attack can lead to a stall. He turned, but not into the wind. Losing speed, treetops getting closer, he pulled back harder. This resulted in a full aerodynamic stall, barely 100 feet off the ground.

Even a quartering wind would have helped the aircraft climb.

Tragically, none of the four pilots survived the crash. The impact was so severe that the engine needed to be dug out of the ground.

This devastating event changed me forever as an instructor. I became adamant about teaching my students to speak up if they see something wrong when flying with others. One voice could have made *all* the difference that day.

The Civil Aviation Safety Authority (CASA) investigated thoroughly, checking the aircraft and the pilots' records. My diligent record-keeping showed I'd done my job. The accident was attributed to human error.

The plane was a total loss. After this heartbreaking incident, I decided it would be the last aircraft I'd own.

Safety *isn't* about rubber stamps or avoiding awkward conversations. It's about *lives*.

Sometimes, the safest thing you can do is say 'No.' If you're in a cockpit and something feels *off*, speak up. Your voice might just save a life.

In aviation, second chances are rare.

CEO Mentality

Flight students come in all shapes and sizes, and attitudes. The ones with CEO mentality are a special breed. They prefer to be in charge, which makes training them... interesting.

As students approach their flight tests, I like to keep them on their toes. Every lesson is a learning experience, even if they have already learned that technique. I wanted to make sure my students are *instinctively* ready, not just book smart.

Enter my CEO student. We'd just finished an instrument manoeuvre when I decided to spice things up. Coming back into Bankstown Airport, I failed his engine. Arms folded; I waited for him to run the drill.

His response was immediate and colourful.

'Why the fuck did you do that, the lesson's over?!' He threw his headset for good measure.

'If I have to take over, you do not fly again,' I warned.

'I'm your fucking customer! You're working for me. I pay your wages!' he blasted.

'If I need to take over, you won't fly again,' I repeated.

Meanwhile, we're losing altitude, and Mr. CEO is still ranting. At 1,500 feet, he finally got the message and ran through the engine restart procedure.

He got the engine started and we climbed back up. He was getting everything ready for landing and about to radio inbound. I failed the engine again.

He absolutely lost his shit.

'This time you're not restarting it,' I informed him. 'We're going to look for somewhere to land. A paddock, runway, your choice.' We were going to practice a forced landing after an engine failure.

He hadn't done a forced landing since he got his initial licence. Unhappy was an understatement.

'You know, time is altitude,' I reminded him helpfully.

'What the fuck?! I just got cleaned up before and now you're doing this?'

'The engine won't start this time. Forced landing it is.'

Over a disused runway in the training area, he ran through the procedures. At 500 feet, I 'fixed' the engine and told him to go around.

He climbed back up and then fiercely guarded the controls so I couldn't touch anything. We came back in and landed.

Back on the ground, he demanded an explanation, stating, 'I don't need to do all that, I already know how to do it!'

During the debrief, he was still fuming.

The next day he came back, apologised, and gave me season tickets to the Waratahs (NSW Rugy Union team).

Justin realised the repeated 'tests' were not for my amusement, but to ensure he was always prepared for the unexpected. I was acutely aware that Justin's future passengers would not be anonymous faces, but his cherished family and friends.

Later, Justin started his own aviation company, and I became his Chief Pilot.

From student to boss, he became one of the most upstanding people I've met.

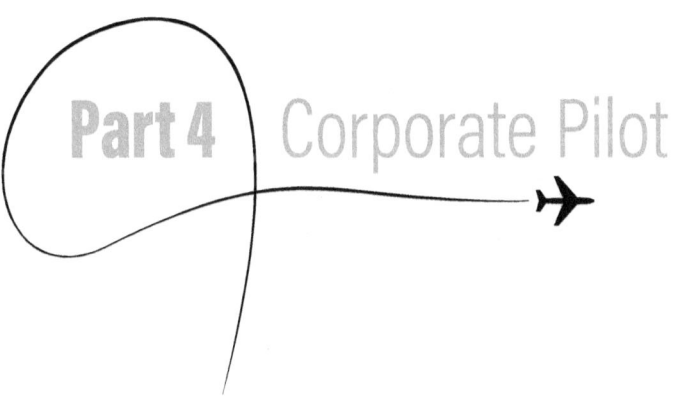

Part 4   Corporate Pilot

'There are no old bold pilots'
- E Hamilton Lee

Mayday Mayday! 6 Souls Onboard

Life has a funny way of flipping the script. One day, you're teaching a student to fly; the next, he's your boss at a private charter company! That's how I found myself flying to Adelaide from Sydney in a Piper Navajo with Justin, his wife, and three fully grown Alsatians.

I was his Chief Pilot, and he was flying his 8-seater twin engine aircraft on a beautiful clear day.

The Navajo's a bit of a workhorse, and the Adelaide route is tricky. With legal fuel reserves, you're just scraping into Adelaide. We always used Mildura as our Point of No Return (PNR). Get there with favourable winds, you're golden. If not, it's refuel time.

Approaching Mildura, I decided to spice things up, rather than just sitting there fat, dumb and happy (it's an expression, he is certainly *not* fat or dumb). Just because Justin was now my boss didn't mean he couldn't continue learning.

'Justin. What would be your Mayday call if we needed to do an emergency landing somewhere?' I asked.

He ran though his Mayday call: aircraft type; aircraft rego; position; altitude; his intention, and location. He then added, 'Six souls on board.'

On the plane there was Justin, his wife Delia, me, and his 3 Alsatians.

I couldn't let that slide. 'No Justin there are 3 souls on board and 3 dogs.'

'But they're like my children, they are my family,' he protested.

'Justin, if you say 6 souls on board, and they only find 3 of us, they'll think each dog ate a person and they'll be put down!'

Justin's wife, Delia, was a nervous flyer. I have found that the fear of flying is often based on not knowing what is going on. So, I made an offer.

Justin had been having some health problems, so I said to Delia, 'Why don't you let me teach you some of the basics, so that you know what to do in an emergency?'

I was thinking radio usage, GPS basics, maybe even landing.

'I don't want to learn how to fly the plane,' she said. 'If we get into trouble, I would prefer just to go down with the plane.'

'Oi!' piped Justin, 'I could just be out of breath!'

Thankfully, our journey to Adelaide remained uneventful, with no need for emergency calls or impromptu flying lessons. The flight proved transformative in an unexpected way, though. What started with Delia's reluctant agreement to learn radio basics blossomed into genuine curiosity. On subsequent flights, she began learning the names and purposes of various flight controls and switches, while Justin, perhaps inspired by our earlier teaching dynamic, started narrating his actions as he flew. Fear gradually gave way to understanding. That nervous passenger who once declared she'd "rather go down with the plane" was slowly transforming into an engaged copilot.

Lake Cargelligo

As Chief Pilot for Avant Air, I often found myself flying for the Royal Flying Doctor Service.

I was flying doctors on a weekly rotation to Bathurst, Orange, Parkes and then Lake Cargelligo in our Piper Navajo. Lake Cargelligo is a small town with a dirt airstrip and a hospital, just west of Parkes. The walk into town was only 2 kilometres and, as this was a very long day, I was allocated a bed for 'day rest' in the hospital.

A bed in a hospital can be very noisy, so thankfully on this trip, I was given a bed in the Domestic Violence House, a private lodging which is more secure. It was quieter, however my nap was cut short due to them needing the bed.

I took a walk around the town and after lunch headed out to the airport to hang around. There was no terminal, just a shed near my plane. As I approached the aircraft, I noticed it was sitting at a weird angle. Getting closer, I realised the left main wheel strut was slightly compressed and collapsing. Pink hydraulic fluid was spurting out of the line attached to the undercarriage.

I ran towards the plane, thinking there was no engineering or aircraft mechanic out here, and nothing I could do. I tried to stop the flow of the corrosive liquid, but my attempt was in vain. The undercarriage banged down onto the wheel.

I couldn't fly like this—it would destroy the undercarriage on the rough dirt runway.

I still had a few hours before the first doctor was due back, before we were to retrace our path and pick up the other doctors from Parkes, Orange, Bathurst and then Sydney. I needed a solution, and fast.

There was a Cessna 172 sitting in the small shed, and I checked to see if there was any way of identifying the owner. I couldn't find anything, though I remembered seeing a service station (petrol station) halfway to the airport. I ran the kilometre back to that station and asked if the attendant knew who owned the Cessna and whether they were a mechanic or engineer. The owner wasn't either, getting his aircraft maintained in Parkes.

I rang my engineer back in Sydney, however with my flip phone's bad reception, I couldn't send photos of the damage. The engineer said we'd need to fly someone out there in a couple of days or ship it back to Sydney on a truck. Neither option was acceptable for me. We had lots of flights booked over the following days.

That's when the helpful attendant at the service station offered a lift back to the airport and said he'd bring a couple of mates to have a look. Before I knew it, we had a group of locals ready to help, complete with tea, coffee, and sandwiches.

As they arrived with tools and gathered around to inspect the damaged undercarriage, I realised this was exactly the kind of situation my 'Lady MacGyver' thinking was made for. It wasn't about having all the answers; it was about staying calm, being resourceful, and working together to find a practical solution with whatever we had on hand.

We all studied the aircraft to determine what we could do.

It was determined that if we could jack up the wing to extend the undercarriage, we might be able to prop it up somehow.

I wasn't willing to retract the undercarriage in flight, so I calculated the fuel needed to fly with it down.

Again, I rang the engineers in Sydney to run our plan by them. They were hesitant, saying it might work but they couldn't guarantee it, stating they wouldn't be liable if the undercarriage collapsed.

One of the men sourced some tools and a 44-gallon drum. We used tyres on the drum to prop up the wing to the height we needed.

To avoid cracking the housing or wheel collar, we used an inner tube on the strut and split some hard plastic plumbing conduit as a cuff. These were then all tied together with metal hose clamps – a makeshift repair that we hoped would hold. I took some photos on my flip phone for future reference and called the engineer in Sydney again. He stayed on the phone while we all held up the wing and slowly removed the tyres and drum. The strut held.

I was willing to fly the aircraft, but I wasn't prepared to fly the doctors with the makeshift repair.

I called the flying doctor service to inform them the aircraft was unable to take them back. They arranged for the doctors to catch taxis to Parkes and then regional flights back to Sydney.

The doctor at Lake Cargelligo, an aviation enthusiast, asked to fly back with me instead. I explained it was no longer a charter flight and wouldn't be covered by insurance. He wrote a waiver stating he was traveling as a private passenger and understood the risks. He was an adventurer like me.

I informed the engineers in Sydney I'd need them at the airport when I landed. Despite their initial reluctance due to it being after hours, they agreed after I explained I was flying back at my own risk as a favour to everyone.

I did a couple of taxi runs on the rough dirt runway to make sure the repair would hold, especially during take-off. Each run, I increased the speed to simulate actual conditions.

After the practise runs, we inspected our repairs, and were satisfied it was going to hold.

The owner of the Cessna offered me fuel from his barrel, which I gratefully accepted. I sent him a cheque once I was back in Sydney.

We took off, keeping the undercarriage down the entire flight, not willing to retract it just in case it got stuck. Flying this way was very slow, and we lost daylight enroute; I made sure to stay above the minimum safe altitude.

For landing, I kept a little power on, so we'd fly onto the runway rather than doing a power-off landing. I held my breath during the entire approach and touchdown.

The engineers met us and seemed surprised by my concern. The aircraft stayed in that condition for the next week until they could properly fix it. Word had spread around the airport, with a few people coming to see our bush repair job.

I made sure to send not just the fuel payment, but also some beer and flowers to the wonderful people of Lake Cargelligo who had helped me. Their community spirit and willingness to help a stranger was truly heartwarming.

For me this experience reinforced the value of quick thinking, teamwork, and the incredible resourcefulness of country folks. It's a reminder that sometimes, the best solutions come from quite unexpected places and people.

In aviation, as in life, a bit of ingenuity and a lot of community spirit can get you through almost anything.

FO or FA?

I arrived early for the charter flight, as usual, and completed the preflight checks. Our passengers were five Japanese businessmen who had just stepped off an international flight. When they saw me in my pilot uniform, their eyes lit up. Being 6 feet tall, blonde, and a pilot, apparently made me the perfect recipe for photos. We lined up next to the aircraft, and I smiled through a flurry of camera clicks.

Once airborne, I discovered the charter company's expectation: I wasn't just one of the pilots, but also the Flight Attendant on the trip.

There I was, stepping out of my pilot seat to serve the coffee, tea, miso soup and catering boxes. On descent, I was cleaning the cabin.

This wasn't a one-off gig. I played this dual role on three other flights. Each time, the company tried to cut costs by having me share a room with the male pilot. I politely declined. If I'm pulling double duty, Flight Officer and Flight Attendant, I deserve my own room.

These experiences taught me that in aviation, you sometimes wear multiple hats; however there is justifiable importance in setting boundaries.

I may be flexible, but I draw the line at compromising my privacy.

We Want a Man

As Chief Pilot for Avant Air at Bankstown Airport, I'd seen my fair share of interesting passengers. We had four pilots, and it was my job to ensure their ongoing proficiency, and the airworthiness of our aircraft.

Nothing quite prepared me for the day Misogyny decided to book a charter flight.

Justin, the owner of the charter company, had received a booking for five executives to fly to Bonville, in Coffs Harbour, home to Australia's most beautiful golf course. I arrived early to prepare for the flight.

The executives turned up with their golf clubs and luggage. I welcomed them in full pilot uniform and then started weighing their luggage, making flight preparations.

Justin was there to help, since our other pilots were already flying other charters.

One of the executives; overweight, middle-aged, and balding, looked around and asked, 'Where's the pilot?'

I stepped forward. 'It's me".

He looked me up and down, smirked and said, 'No. Really. Where's the pilot?'

By now, we had an audience. The other execs gathered round, observing the unfolding drama.

Justin intervened, 'Michelle is our Chief Pilot, and also our best pilot.'

Old mate then said, 'No. We want a *real* pilot.'

I explained that the other pilots were already flying, reiterating that I would be their pilot.

He responded, 'If we can't get a real pilot then we aren't going.'

Justin stepped in and restated, 'Michelle is our top pilot. Our Chief Pilot. Just confirming, what you are saying is that if she is your pilot, you are not going?'

'Yes,' came the resolute reply.

Justin smiled and said, 'Well in that case, as you are cancelling your flight within 24 hours you are not eligible for a refund.'

Cue the swearing and carrying on. He maintained his stance about wanting a 'real pilot,' threatened repercussions and left, with none of the other passengers speaking up against his discrimination.

Justin turned to me, apologising for their Stone Age attitudes. 'I can't believe this. I'm sorry that men still have this attitude about female pilots.'

He then asked, 'Where have you always wanted to go for lunch?'

Justin, his wife Delia, and I then used the charter fee and enjoyed a very nice lunch at the beautiful Catalina's at Rose Bay.

I don't know if they have ever played golf at the stunning Bonville, Australia's frequently voted 'Most beautiful' course, but they certainly missed out that day, and all because of their genuinely archaic misogyny.

Thanks for the lunch, Justin, and thank you for paying, old mate.

Ad Man & Cheese

After getting my commercial pilot licence, I trained for my endorsement on the Cessna Citation II, a small business jet. Shortly after, I started picking up work with a couple of companies in Sydney, who had regular clients, one of which was very well known in the advertising industry.

Interestingly, my Mum had worked for him as a receptionist when she was 15, my sister in advertising and marketing roles, and now I was flying him around in a small jet. It was quite the family connection.

I headed out to Sydney Airport to fly a charter for our Ad Man. We had detailed notes for our regular clients, covering everything from their preferred cabin temperature to how they wished to be addressed, catering requirements and any other preferences. We always prepared the flight to meet these specifications.

There were two pilots on this flight, and I was the Co-Pilot. I waited at the bottom of the stairs to greet our passengers. There were four of them: the client and his wife, and two of their guests.

Our client was always happy and jovial when he arrived. He walked up to the plane with a big smile and said, 'Hello Michelle. Gorgeous day for flying isn't it?' He then proceeded up the stairs.

His wife, who was about the same age as me, or only slightly older, looked me up and down, curled her top lip and said, 'Oh, it's you,' and pushed past to climb the stairs. The other two passengers just smiled pleasantly and boarded.

I directed them to the safety cards, exits, then hopped into my seat to start the pre-flight checks.

The flight was from Sydney to King Island, where they were going for lunch. King Island is part of Tasmania, in Bass Strait, and is famous for its produce, particularly their cheese. I'm particularly fond of King Island Brie.

During the flight, I checked to see they had everything they needed and left my seat to help clean up, putting away a couple of empty champagne bottles before we landed.

On the tarmac, I descended the stairs first and told our client and passengers that we would be here when they got back. It was a scheduled two-hour lunch followed by a return flight to Sydney.

After they left, I helped the Captain straighten up the cabin in preparation for their return. We then noticed a distinct smell in the cabin and upon inspection found that our client's wife had smeared Camembert cheese on the window, stuffed more into the seat pocket, and poured champagne around her departing mess.

I wanted to leave the cabin in this state for their return, however the Captain pointed out they were our paying customers and we needed to be professional and clean it up.

We cleaned and tidied the mess, then took a taxi into town to restock with more cheese and champagne for their return flight.

Their lunch ended up taking four and a half hours. When they returned, our client was in very good spirits. He tipped me $200 and hopped up the stairs. His wife, on the other hand, returned even *surlier* than before and proceeded to trip up the stairs. She started on the new champagne and then promptly fell asleep.

When we landed in Sydney, our client tipped me another $200 and offered an apology for his wife's behaviour, him still being very pleasant and jovial.

The cleaning crew complained of the state of the cabin and asked management if an extra fee could be added to the charter. I don't think the company did that; he was a very good returning customer.

After I stopped flying for that company, I heard he had moved on to a more refined lunch partner.

This job taught me to expect the unexpected, even from our most regular clients. It's not always smooth flying, but it certainly keeps things interesting.

Just remember, if you're ever on a private jet, treat it (and your pilot) with respect. You never know when you might need a favour at altitude.

Bottle of Urine at My Head

I'd now flown my fair share of interesting passengers, when a different charter boss asked me to fly his mates to Scone races in rural NSW; I didn't know I was about to experience one of my most dangerous flights.

The morning flight to Scone was standard enough. My passengers were highly respected businessmen heading out for a day at the races. I spent several hours at the small regional airport waiting for their return.

They arrived back riding high on race winnings and what seemed like the contents of the entire Scone Race Club bar. However, their jovial mood deteriorated mid-flight when nature called, and they questioned the location of the (non-existent) toilet. A cursory glance behind them would have been enough to know we didn't have the facilities.

They thought it hilarious to use their empty bottles to relieve themselves. When some of the bottles tipped over, the stench was nauseating.

In a 10-seater twin engine aircraft, even weight distribution is critical. This basic aviation principle was lost on six large, intoxicated men when they decided to play a game of musical chairs at altitude. They stumbled from one side of the aircraft to the other, causing dangerous weight shifts that threatened our stability. Six hefty blokes versus one pilot—the mathematics wasn't in my favour. I had to fight hard to keep control of the aircraft.

I ordered them to sit down. They laughed.

I threatened to land at the nearest airport and leave them to find their own way home.

They responded by launching a urine-filled beer bottle at my head.

The bottle hit my headset, spraying its contents throughout the cockpit.

Enough!

I declared an emergency to air traffic control and diverted to Warnervale. These 'respected businessmen' were met by the police and removed from my aircraft, their dignity left somewhere between the Scone Race Club and the police station.

Sometimes the most dangerous situations don't come from mechanical failures or bad weather, but from the very paying passengers in the aircraft behind you. These men might have been Titans of Industry on the ground, but in the air, they were nothing but dangerous idiots.

Flying Angels

Angel Flight Australia helps rural families connect to vital medical treatment they couldn't otherwise access. Private donations keep the organisation running, with pilots donating their time, skills, and often their aircraft to help those in need. I was proud to be one of those pilots, flying quite a few missions for the organisation.

Among all these flights, one stands out—not for its difficulty, but for showing me the true meaning of grace and community.

A gentleman in his 40s, from Bowen in far north Queensland, had been in Sydney receiving extended treatment for a degenerative disease. His liver and kidneys were failing, he was also blind and slowly losing mobility. Angel Flight contacted me to fly him home. He knew it was the end and wanted to spend his final days in the community where he grew up.

He arrived at Bankstown Airport with a nurse managing his oxygen tank and his beautiful guide dog.

I set him up in the front with me, oxygen bottles carefully rigged up behind him. Despite *everything* he was facing, he was so lovely—chatting and laughing the whole way up. He was the sort of person who never dwelled on his ailments or pain, instead focusing on making others happy. When his condition came up in conversation, he'd just brush it off. He was a natural entertainer.

'When a blind person jumps out of a plane, how do we know when the ground is coming up?' he asked mid-flight.

'I don't know.'

'The leash goes slack,' he chortled.

I'm glad his guide dog couldn't understand his jokes, which kept on coming throughout the flight.

Mid-journey, the nurse tapped my shoulder—we were using more oxygen than calculated due to our altitude. We were getting great tail winds at 10,000 feet, however I descended to extend his oxygen supply. When it became clear we'd still run short, I radioed ahead to Port Macquarie. An ambulance met us with two more oxygen bottles, allowing us to continue safely to Bowen.

The airport in Bowen is small with no control tower. Twenty-five nautical miles out, I made our approach call. The radio frequency was unusually busy. Four other aircraft had joined us, in loose formation, to escort him home. It brought tears to my eyes.

The whole community was awaiting our arrival. The Country Women's Association (CWA) had set up a marquee serving coffee, tea and cakes. They were celebrating his return. When I told him what was happening outside, he cried happy tears. There were big hugs for everyone, including the nurse and me.

I couldn't stay long as I had an early flight the next day. After a final hug, I took off back to Sydney. Once airborne, I couldn't control my tears. I landed at Bankstown at 1am, forever changed by the experience.

I loved donating my time to Angel Flight, receiving *far more* than I gave. To witness someone being remembered and celebrated like that; to see such love from a community—shifted my entire perspective on life.

You just don't know how long you have here on Earth. This gentleman showed me how to leave the world better than you found it; how to have the sort of impact on others that creates lasting memories.

Even in his final days, he was teaching others about grace, humour, and the power of community.

Thank you, sir. I am in no doubt that you are now an Angel yourself.

Lightning is Scary

I discovered, rather dramatically, that the Piper Chieftain, doesn't appreciate lightning.

This lesson came during what started as a routine charter flight from Bankstown to Sydney Airport, then on to Cooma in the Snowy Mountains.

The day had already been long. I'd completed an early morning flight to Coffs Harbour and back, about an hour and a half north of Sydney, before meeting my next passengers.

Weight and balance calculations are crucial in a 10-seater aircraft, so when the family of five—two parents, three children, plus their nanny – arrived at Sydney Airport, laden with ski gear and excess luggage, I knew we had work to do.

Despite my prior warnings about weight limits, it took lengthy negotiations to convince them to cull their baggage. Each item was sparking debate, however safety trumps convenience every time. To accommodate their remaining luggage, I adjusted my flight plan, by reducing fuel, as I could upload the extra required for my return flight, once in Cooma.

Every calculation was precise – the margin for error in a fully loaded Chieftain is slim.

At maximum take-off weight, I requested 16R, the longer runway at Sydney Airport. Our little 10-seater looked rather out of place amongst the large commercial jets. I also requested a long upwind leg to prevent the engines overheating—the Chieftain's engines work hard at maximum weight, and treating them gently pays dividends.

The weather was perfect: a crystal-clear winter's day, and we landed in Cooma without incident. After unloading my passengers for their ski holiday, I refuelled and checked the weather. It was around 5.30pm, dusk, settling in, with clear conditions forecast for my return flight to Bankstown Airport.

Cooma's wildlife presents its own challenges. Before take-off, I needed to taxi up and down the runway several times to clear it of the kangaroos. They're particularly fond of the twilight hours, and a Roo-Strike was the *last* thing I needed.

Night flying has always been a favourite activity of mine. The stars shine brighter, radio chatter quietens, and the air smooths out. Coastal thunderstorms create spectacular light shows in the clouds. This night seemed particularly clear as I cruised at 9,000 feet.

I'd flown this route countless times to Cooma, Jindabyne, and Polo Flat around the ski fields. Early on in my career, I'd made a conscious decision to avoid complacency. Rather than following the same path each time (the aforementioned magenta line), I varied my route, learning different landmarks, committing each detail to memory. I knew every radio frequency by heart, every control step, where to stay in or out of controlled airspace, and the lowest safe altitudes for each section.

The Great Dividing Range had become my familiar companion, running roughly parallel to Australia's east coast. It's the longest single mountain range existing in one country and the fifth-longest land-based mountain chain globally. Sometimes I would do visual departures for passengers, giving them spectacular views of this ancient landscape.

This intimate knowledge of the terrain would prove invaluable.

Ahead, I could see Sydney's lights glowing on the horizon. A single, thin sliver of cloud hung in the otherwise clear sky, appearing no more than about 500 feet thick. The weather radar showed nothing of concern—just a benign wisp in an otherwise clear night.

I entered the cloud, flying IFR (Instrument Flight Rules). Flying IMC—Instrument Meteorological Conditions—requires pilots to rely primarily on instruments rather than visual references.

A deafening *Bang!* shook the entire aircraft.

Every instrument went black. The cockpit plunged into darkness. All radio communication ceased.

The weather phenomenon known as St Elmo's fire danced across my windscreen—a violet, luminous electrical discharge from the charged atmosphere; like those plasma globes where electricity reaches for your finger, but this was Mother Nature's version, playing across my windscreen in the darkness.

The turbulence tossed the aircraft violently; the autopilot had disengaged with the shock. I struggled to keep my eyes focused on the horizon.

Training took over. First priority: ensure aircraft control, check for immediate threats.

The Chieftain was stable and flying but the instruments were dead.

To get out of this mess safely, I needed a plan.

Despite what most people assume, there's usually time for decision-making during emergencies in the air. Generally speaking, unless you're on fire, out of fuel, or missing a wing, you have as much time as your fuel allows.

I knew my location and time since take-off, so I maintained heading and altitude until I could safely descend from the cloud. The Chieftain's unpressurised cabin meant I couldn't climb above the weather—we were limited to 10,000 feet.

Unsure if my radio was functioning, I set my transponder to 7600 – the radio failure code.

We use a mnemonic for these codes: 77 going to heaven (emergency), 76 radio tricks (radio failure), 75 staying alive (hijacking).

What I didn't realise then was that 7600 triggered a national broadcast—every Air Traffic Controller in the *country* knew of my situation.

I transmitted blind, making radio calls without hearing responses, including on the emergency frequency 121.50.

Still in the cloud, I announced my intended descent, estimated position, heading and altitude—all educated guesses without working instruments.

I tried calling the ATIS on my mobile to get weather and other aerodrome information but couldn't get any service. The Automatic Terminal Information Service would have given me crucial details about conditions at Bankstown, but I was on my own.

Fighting turbulence while hand-flying the aircraft, I finally broke through the cloud, just above Camden, further east than expected, but safely above minimum safe altitudes.

I knew my way to Bankstown from here and continued broadcasting my intentions.

I flew over Bankstown Airport and, after checking for traffic, completed a circuit and landed safely.

The adrenalin had kept me going, but sitting there after shutdown, reality hit. The Piper Chieftain's limitations had put me in a vulnerable position—no pressurisation meant no escape route above the weather, and single-pilot operations meant no one to share the load, or troubleshoot with, in emergencies.

A police car arrived, lights flashing.

The officer jumped out and said, 'You have to cancel your SAR watch!'

The 7600 code had triggered the national Search And Rescue alert. Though they could see I'd landed at Bankstown Airport, protocol demanded I *officially* cancel it.

'I'm obviously here,' I told the officer.

'Yeah, but you have to *call* them,' he explained.

I rang the number to cancel the search and rescue. The operator chided me: 'Ma'am, you should know that this goes national, so you shouldn't use it unless you need it.'

'I did need it! I was in controlled airspace with no instruments,' I responded firmly.

After submitting the incident paperwork, I resolved to seek *bigger* aircraft to fly. Something pressurised, with the capability to climb above weather, rather than through it. Something that came with a second pilot, so next time I faced an emergency, I'd have a colleague beside me, instead of relying solely my own reflection.

But most importantly, this experience reinforced the value of thorough preparation and local knowledge. My habit of varying routes and learning the terrain intimately had given me the tools to handle this emergency. Sometimes, the best emergency equipment is the knowledge in your head.

Time for something bigger, I thought. These 'bug smashers' had taught me well, but it was time to move up.

Looking back at that night over the Snowy Mountains, I realised I unconsciously followed a pattern that would later become my SOAR method (Stop, Observe, Adjust, Rise). When the lightning struck and the instruments went dark, my first action was to Stop and breathe—fighting panic wouldn't keep us in the air. I Observed my situation: location, fuel state, weather conditions. Then came Adjustment—calculating a safe descent path without instruments. Finally, Rise above the challenge, using knowledge of the terrain to navigate home safely.

Sometimes our best learning comes from our most challenging moments. That night taught me far more than just following emergency procedures; it showed me how to turn obstacles into opportunities.

Rex Interview

After two years as Chief Pilot for a couple of charter companies, I was ready for the next step in my career. A rostered position in an airline. This would give my son, my parents and me much more stability. I had enjoyed all the adventure till now, but needed more from my career.

With my flying hours, experience, and connection to the land from my cotton farming days, I set my sights on regional airlines. Rex was my first choice among the three options available on the East Coast: Eastern Airlines and Sunstate Airlines, now both operated under Qantaslink.

I submitted applications to all of them but heard nothing for months.

That's when serendipity stepped in. Tim, whom I knew from my instructing days at Bankstown Airport, worked in Rex operations but wanted to return to flying. Not just as a line pilot—he wanted management. An idea formed.

I valued my relationships at the charter company and wanted to leave on good terms. Finding a suitable replacement for myself seemed the perfect solution. I proposed a deal to Tim: if he could secure me an interview—just an *interview*, not a job—at Rex, I'd recommend him as my replacement in the charter company. He agreed.

That afternoon, after Tim placed my resume on both the HR Manager's and Chief Pilot's desks, I got the call. Tim became the charter company's new Chief Pilot, and I had my interview with Rex.

The timing was perfect. Airlines were expanding rapidly, with Virgin just starting up. Regional airlines were losing pilots to Qantas and Virgin, while other aviators headed overseas. I turned to 'PPRuNe' —the professional pilot rumour mill—for insight. These online forums offered technical discussions, interview tips, and crucially, information about Rex's simulator check in the Metroliner, which made me smile. I had over 500 hours flying in an old Metroliner II, without a reliable autopilot; hand-flying and needing to trim constantly. Training in a difficult aircraft had prepared me well for flying one that actually worked properly.

I arrived at the Melbourne interview sweating profusely, joining 3 other candidates in reception—all men, one particularly confident about his chances. When called in, they suggested I remove my jacket for comfort. Thanks to those forum tips, I kept my jacket on, despite the heat. Later in my career, sitting on interview panels myself, I confirmed this was indeed a recruitment technique to test professionalism.

Facing the Chief Pilot, General Manager, and Head of HR, I handled their standard questions comfortably. Then came their curve ball: 'Pretend we're at a BBQ. I know nothing about flying. Please explain to me P-Force in twin-engine aircraft.'

My Grade 1 instructor-experience kicked in. I asked to use props (found in the tearoom) and proceeded to arrange the table. Barbecue sauce and tomato sauce became engines, while knives and forks represented P-Force and P-Factor. I explained engine failure scenarios, contra-rotating effects, and performance implications.

Their laughter could have meant anything, positive or negative, but they praised my creative use of condiments and cutlery.

The simulator check paired me with another applicant. Comfortable in the left seat from my Metroliner experience, I took the Captain's position while he settled into the right seat. The simulator check Captain had my colleague go first: take-off, circuit at 5,000 feet, engine failure, and single-engine ILS approach with strong crosswind. I supported with radio calls and gear/flap selection as needed.

When my turn came, the simulator felt luxurious compared to my usual Metro. The familiar trim beeping that often distracted less familiar pilots was like background music to me. The check Captain, noticing my comfort, failed my other engine and increased turbulence.

Even with heightened turbulence, I maintained precise control, scanning the six-pack of instruments in a natural flow. Time seemed to slow as everything clicked into place. Then he cranked up the crosswind beyond the aircraft's certified maximum.

I started laughing. 'I wouldn't land now because the crosswind exceeds what the aircraft is capable of,' I explained. 'Especially on one engine.'

He smiled, reduced the crosswind to maximum limits, and completed the landing, still chuckling.

'I've never had anyone do that. Laugh at the same time, during their check. So, you're pretty confident?' he questioned.

'No, no. I don't want to come across as *over*confident. It was just so much more extreme than I expected. I didn't think it would be like this,' I explained.

'It was fun,' he replied. 'You'll fit in well here at Rex.'

Later, as I waited for my taxi, the Chief Pilot shook my hand. 'Thank you for coming in for the interview. We'll see you in a couple of weeks.'

The official letter was just a formality—I knew I'd made it.

I was going to be an airline pilot.

Part 5 REX First Officer

'In flying, you need at least two of these things: altitude, speed, or brains.' - *Chuck Yeager*

Pilot Crash Pad

Ground school in Sydney was the first step in my airline career—intensive training on aircraft systems, engine management, approach procedures, and company standards. The technical aspects were challenging, but I was now close to my little boy. Training in Sydney meant I could maintain our family routine, even if study consumed most of my waking hours.

The next stage would test us as a family. My Training Captain was based in Wagga Wagga, 460 kilometres from Sydney. I moved there after completing my simulator training and endorsement, while my son stayed with Mum. I'd make the journey back every weekend, a painful but necessary arrangement. The promise was six months, then a transfer back to Sydney.

My Training Captain embodied perfectionism. His unsmiling demeanour and unspoken (and spoken) demand for 100% excellence meant I didn't need to criticise myself—he handled that thoroughly. Each flight was a lesson in precision, each debrief an exercise in attention to detail. I respected his approach; it accelerated my learning.

During a rare overnight stay, we found ourselves at the hotel bar after the last sector. The conversation turned to my past life, teaching welding. For the first time, I saw him animated. He wanted to build umpire chairs for his tennis court. Our remaining training flights were filled with detailed discussions about metal types, equipment specifications, and construction plans.

He purchased the exact amount of material required—no room for error, typical of his precise nature.

'Maybe a bit of scrap is required so I can show you how to do it?' I suggested.

'You do the first one, and I will copy you,' he replied.

After we created two perfect umpire chairs, his flight instructions, while still demanding perfection, carried a softer edge. We'd found common ground beyond the cockpit.

With training complete, I became a line First Officer, but my living situation presented new challenges.

To save money, I shared accommodation with four younger male pilots in their early 20s. Their idea of housekeeping differed vastly from mine. Empty pizza boxes decorated the living room, and the kitchen sink regularly overflowed with dishes. As a mum focused on saving money and maximising time with my son, I avoided their parties; they would often bring young ladies back home and coincidentally my makeup and other toiletries would mysteriously disappear from the bathroom.

I contributed to beer funds, playing my part in the 'Boys' Club' I'd chosen to join. The only other female pilot in Wagga, married to a Captain, and with a young family, kept to herself. I understood why—balancing family *and* flying required careful time management.

When the promised six-month mark arrived without a Sydney-based transfer, I approached HR. Their responses was blunt: 'You're going to have to suck it up because that's how it is.'

Their stance wasn't entirely unreasonable. At the time Rex were haemorrhaging pilots to Virgin, Jetstar, and Qantas, leaving little flexibility for our Base preferences. Every month brought news of another pilot heading to the major airlines. After several more months, the separation from my son became untenable.

I approached the Chief Pilot with an ultimatum: transfer to Sydney or accept my resignation. This wasn't a hollow threat at all—I was prepared to repay the $28,000 training bond required if pilots left within a designated period. The company had invested in our training and needed to protect that investment, but I needed to protect my *relationship* with my young son.

The Training Captain—my former welding student—said he would help make it work. Within six weeks, I was back in Sydney with my son.

Sometimes the strongest professional bonds form over the simplest shared interests, and sometimes standing firm, for what matters most, brings unexpected allies.

One of the Boys

Early in my aviation career I sensed an unspoken rule: you need to be 'one of the boys' if you are to succeed.

My first lesson came before I even had my licence. The flying school had asked me to work at their stand at the local flying show. I arrived in a fitted navy skirt and pilot shirt—professional behind the display, but problematic everywhere else.

When I was invited that day to look inside a Beach 1900's flight deck—significantly larger than anything I'd flown—I discovered the limitations of the skirt. Getting into the First Officer's seat required hiking the fabric up to manage the step over. Several onlookers sat back and watched my awkward manoeuvre with obvious amusement. After then, and my Pacific crossing, trousers became my permanent choice of uniform.

The industry's attitude towards female pilots resulted in degrading airport 'jokes' about sexual favours being our pathway to employment. How degrading and insulting to insinuate this was our professional behaviour, however survival meant adapting to the male-dominated environment. Airlines had few female pilots, and those who made it, learned to adjust.

Male colleagues offered their 'helpful' advice: wear minimal makeup; offer no please or thank you when requesting crew coffee (I ignored that one); smile infrequently; pull hair back severely. Don't mention children or anything 'female-specific'. Wear trousers.

Even footwear sparked controversy. My RM Williams boots, with a modest Cuban heel, drew criticism from colleagues, and one passenger declared they should be illegal for female pilots.

These weren't just suggestions—they were unwritten rules of acceptance. To succeed in aviation, you didn't just need to fly well; you needed to also navigate this complex terrain of gender expectations.

Victor the Trickster

Early days in Australian aviation saw a culture of playful rivalry between pilots and cabin crew. Nothing that compromised safety, just pranks that built camaraderie. When I started airline flying, I'd hear tales from the TAA and Ansett days, never expecting to experience these hijinks myself.

In those earlier days, cabin crew made sandwiches from scratch—not the pre-packaged versions of today. They'd slice fresh tomatoes and arrange the ham, preparing meals in the galley between services. This hands-on food prep created endless opportunities for mischief.

The flight crew grew accustomed to receiving coffee with suspicious additions: excessive sugar, salt instead of sugar, eye drops with their notorious laxative effect, and reportedly, even expressed breast milk. Pilots, in those times, learned to be wary of anything arriving in the cockpit, studying each offering like bomb disposal experts.

One infamous story involved seemingly innocent ham and tomato sandwiches. When their sandwiches arrived that day, they studied the stewardess's expression carefully before taking tentative bites. Finding nothing immediately amiss, just slightly chewy bread, they finished their meal under her watchful eye.

'How were the sandwiches?' she enquired, maintaining perfect composure.

'Good,' they replied, watching her smile as she left the cockpit.

Later, their suspicions mounting, they questioned her about the sandwiches. The truth emerged: she'd constructed them with bread, a layer of butter, a sheet of toilet paper, which slowly dissolved into the butter, followed by another sheet, and another, then ham and tomato, until a total of 7 sheets of toilet paper had been absorbed by the butter. The chewiness, that they'd attributed to stale bread, wasn't.

The pilots got their revenge during an overnight stay. While the stewardesses enjoyed a swim in the hotel pool, the pilots snuck into their rooms, adjusted their clocks, and placed their water-soaked underwear in the freezer.

Next morning, after a frantic search for their undergarments and a late call from reception, the flustered stewardesses boarded the crew bus in full uniform, triangles of darker fabric betraying their frozen, drenched state.

My personal experience with aviation pranks came from Victor, a Captain I flew with at Rex, and later, Virgin Australia. His handlebar moustache and deadpan expression were legendary, matched only by his reputation for mischief. Every flight with Victor promised entertainment, though you *never* knew quite where it would come from.

We were operating a 36-seater SAAB: Captain Victor, me as First Officer, and a particularly inexperienced cabin crew member. The SAAB's compact flight deck made for intimate working conditions, perfect for Victor's brand of theatre.

When our new crew member offered lunch and coffee, Victor orchestrated his performance with the imagination and precision of a symphony conductor.

'Keep your hands on the control column, look straight ahead, and just run with it,' he instructed me quietly, his moustache twitching slightly with anticipated amusement.

When she returned with my coffee, Victor intervened. 'Michelle can't take it because she's flying.'

'Ahh OK, what do I do with it?' she asked, confusion evident in her voice.

'You'll have to come in and help her take a drink,' Victor declared, face perfectly serious. Years of practice had perfected his poker face.

I could sense her mental review of training modules that hadn't covered hand-feeding pilots. Her professionalism wavered with uncertainty.

As she raised the cup to my lips, Victor exclaimed, 'Whoa, you'll have to blow on it first, it'll burn her!' She obligingly cooled my coffee while I struggled to maintain composure, my knuckles whitening on the control column.

The sandwich presented new opportunities for Victor's direction.

'She'll choke! You'll have to break some off for her.'

Our new crew member dutifully broke off small pieces, feeding me like a baby bird while Victor found endless reasons to exclaim, 'Whoa, whoa!' and add new requirements to the process.

I called a halt after a few bites, unable to maintain composure any longer. Victor dissolved into laughter once she'd left, his handlebar moustache quivering with mirth.

His pranks weren't limited to the air. On overnight stays, he'd convince crew members that ironing his shirts was part of their duties. He claimed a 50% success rate with this particular stunt, proudly displaying his crisp uniforms as evidence.

While I oppose bullying and mockery, Victor had an innate ability to read people and situations. His goal was never to humiliate, but to create shared moments of pure absurdity. This distinction—between laughing *at* someone and laughing *with* them—was a crucial lesson to learn working within the male-dominated airline industry.

Learning to become 'one of the guys' meant understanding a culture previously unknown to me, including this tradition of practical jokes and shared laughter. It was about building connections through humour—not creating divisions. Victor's antics, while perhaps sometimes a little outrageous, always served to bring the crew closer together.

His approach taught me valuable lessons about leadership and team building. Sometimes the strongest bonds form not through *formal* processes but through shared experiences and *laughter*.

Victor was a master at walking that line between authority and approachability, using humour to bridge the gap.

Captain, my Captain

After 18 months as a First Officer (FO) at Rex Airlines, I got the tap on the shoulder for my command upgrade. At most airlines, becoming a Captain works on seniority. Keep your flying record clean; wait your turn.

With Rex losing pilots to larger airlines with bigger jets and *better pay*, my number came up sooner than it might have at a major airline.

The journey to four stripes started with intense study—if you don't like hitting the books, aviation isn't your field. The pre-course preparation was comprehensive: aircraft systems, emergency procedures, company policies and regulatory requirements. Everything needed to be second nature before ground school even began.

Three days of ground school followed, drilling deeper into the responsibilities of command. The technical knowledge was just the beginning—they needed to know we could handle the decision-making, the crew management and the responsibility for *every* aspect of the flight.

Then came simulator training in the left-hand seat. The captain's seat demanded learning everything anew—different hand positions, different responsibilities, and the added task of taxiing the aircraft. What had become natural from the right seat now felt awkward and reversed. Even simple tasks required my conscious thought.

I trained alongside another pilot of similar seniority, an experience that initially seemed like preferential treatment was being bestowed upon him. Our Training Captain would ignore my questions, directing all responses to my male colleague. I assumed he disliked female pilots, but later learnt he actually had issues with my colleague, constantly trying to catch him out.

After passing initial training then came 'line' training—flying as the Captain with the Training Captain in the First Officer's seat. This however meant another six-week separation from my son; I was based in Adelaide, South Australia. The sacrifices I made for those stripes kept mounting, but the goal was *worth* it.

The final hurdle was the simulator check in Melbourne. Everyone knew the script: engine failures, fires, the usual emergencies, but the real key to success lay in your paired First Officer. They could make or break your command upgrade.

When I learnt who I'd been rostered with, relief washed over me. He was the most experienced First Officer for check flights, known for his professionalism and capability. I called him immediately, suggesting drinks the day before.

Over a beer at the airport, I played to his expertise. 'You are the best FO when it comes to doing this check, better than any Captain. You can do it with your eyes closed,' I told him. 'Could I ask you a favour?'

'Sure.'

'Because you know it so well, better than any Captain, can you let me take charge and only speak up if I'm clearly missing something or heading down the wrong path?'

'No problem.'

He then shared invaluable tips about common pitfalls, appreciating the respect I'd shown for his experience. He warned me about specific emergency scenarios that often tripped up candidates and suggested ways to stay ahead of the aircraft during critical phases.

On the day, during the check, he was perfect—supportive but letting me lead. His quiet competence allowed me to demonstrate my command ability without interference. The check Captain declared it one of the best checks he'd seen.

We celebrated with airport beers before catching a Virgin flight back to Sydney. Running on minimal sleep, those drinks went straight to my head. Landing in Sydney, the Rex base manager waited to present my Captain's epaulettes.

Four stripes never felt so good.

The next day, I was rostered as Captain. I appreciated the company's approach—scheduling new Captains *immediately* after their check showed faith in our abilities, even if it added a touch more pressure.

That first take-off from the left seat as commander felt *different*. The view wasn't just different physically; it represented years of work, sacrifice, and determination.

Importantly, this journey taught me that success often comes down to respecting the experience of others and knowing when to ask for help. Sometimes the best leadership starts with acknowledging expertise in others.

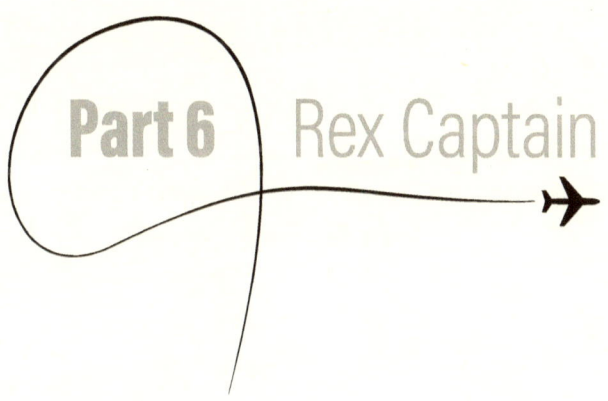
Part 6　Rex Captain

'Aviation is not so much a profession as it is a disease.' -
Dr Paul Garber

Drunk FO

An easy Saturday morning lay ahead. A run from Sydney to Dubbo and then done for the day, all before lunch.

I arrived around 5.15am, for a 5.45am sign on. I switched on the crew room lights and started reviewing the weather and flight plan.

The Flight Attendant arrived promptly, but our First Officer was nowhere to be seen. I ran through the briefing with our Flight Attendant, covering memory items—the emergency procedures you needed to know by heart, required review every seven days. He was professional, clearly still building his confidence, but thorough with every procedure.

After calling crewing about our missing First Officer, they said he was running late and would meet us at the aircraft. Not ideal, but manageable. We walked out to the aircraft, and I completed the walk-around, getting everything ready.

Still no First Officer.

Usually, the First Officer handles the flight plan loading, weight and balance calculations, and passenger boarding.

Fifteen minutes late, he finally appeared. Our 30-minute pre-flight window had shrunk considerably, though we could still make up time in the air.

His first words set the tone. Seeing our male Flight Attendant: 'Oh fuck, I'm here with a Queen!'

Then, entering the cockpit: 'Oh fuck, my day got even worse, a bloody woman!'

The Flight Attendant and I exchanged glances, we both raised one eyebrow. I told the FO the aircraft was ready and that he still needed to do the weight and balance sheet and grab the passengers. He went off to do it.

The Flight Attendant was clearly upset and asked, 'Seriously, what is his problem?'

'Try not to worry about him, he's clearly not a nice person,' I replied. 'It's only 2 sectors, we don't have to be with him for long.'

The FO came back with the passengers and was clearly still grumpy. His communication was short; he would only say the bare minimum. He called the checklist—not per standard operating procedures—a very cursory mention of different items. He'd basically done a shorthand version of the checklist.

I pulled him up on it and said, 'No, we need to do it again, properly.'

He reluctantly ran through it again and we taxied onto the runway.

I told him I would be flying the first sector out to Dubbo, and we climbed to cruising height. The FO kept missing radio calls so Sydney Air Traffic Control kept calling us and I needed to keep prompting the FO: 'That was us.'

The flight to Dubbo is only a short hop, and when I looked over at him, he had his eyes closed with his head leaning against the window. I asked him if he was tired.

'Yeah, I was out all night. I had a big one. It was a massive bender, and I only got home half an hour before I had to come to work,' he replied.

This gave me grave concern, especially after I noticed he'd fallen asleep.

I did the radio, his job, as we flew closer to the destination. I touched his elbow to wake him and told him we needed to do our briefing as we approached Dubbo.

'You've done this before, you don't need me,' he said.

'I do actually,' I replied, 'and you need to do your tasks as well.'

As we started our descent, he burped, and his breath stank of alcohol. I opened the gasper to get some fresh air around me, and I asked, 'How much did you have to drink?'

'I was shitfaced,' he casually replied.

There are very strict rules in aviation. Back in the early days of aviation there was a saying: '8 hours from bottle to throttle,' however, zero alcohol in your system is the rule now, with zero tolerance.

He was not being very nice, he was not answering calls and telling me to do them, claiming he was too tired.

We landed in Dubbo. Usually, the FO goes into the terminal and calculates the weight and balance for the return leg, and then brings out the passengers, whilst the Captain does the walkaround and resets the onboard computer. However this time, I told him I would go in to do the weight and balance and get the passengers. I told him to do the walk around.

I went inside to think. *What am I going to do here?*

I called my base manager and informed him of the situation and how I didn't feel confident taking him back as my operating crew to Sydney.

I didn't want to cancel the flight and impact the passengers, so I asked if there was anyone already in Dubbo who could fly with me. There was another pilot who could come in; they were an hour away. In my mind that was OK, the delay wouldn't be too long for the passengers. We had a solution.

A little while later, my manager called me back and asked, 'Why do you think the FO is unfit to fly?'

'I don't really want to get him into trouble, I just don't feel he is fit to fly,' I hesitantly responded.

'No, you need to tell me now,' was the instruction.

I told him what the FO had told me about coming home shitfaced 30 minutes before sign-on, his attitude, his actions *and lack of* actions, and the alcohol burp from hell.

'OK, well he is grounded,' my base manager informed me.

I went out and told the terminal staff the flight was delayed.

I walked out to the aircraft and noticed the Flight Attendant was outside. He had received more snide comments from the FO and didn't want to be inside with him. He told me he didn't think he could even do this last sector with him. This comment helped me come to terms with what was about to happen. I told him to stand by because we had a delay.

I went into the aircraft and spoke to the FO about what was going to happen, that he was grounded. He swore at me. Threatened me. Asked me if it was 'that time of the month,' and why I couldn't take a joke. He stormed off to the terminal.

My base manager had called the local police who met him in the terminal where he was breathalysed. The reading indicated he wasn't fit to even drive a car. Certainly not the zero-alcohol required to fly.

He was arrested and subsequently lost his job.

Sunshine Every Day

As an airline Captain, I discovered one of my life's purposes: contribution. Some chase goals for achievement or recognition, but I found my greatest satisfaction was helping others reach *theirs*.

We pilots have a unique privilege: sunshine every day. No matter what's happening below; above the clouds the sun *always* shines. In summer, we'd climb through grey storm clouds into brilliant light. During winter, we'd rise above the gloom into a perfect blue sky. That daily ascent became my reset button.

Walking through the airport carpark, life's usual stresses—sick kids, bills, relationship tangles—would fade, as I shifted into 'work Michelle'. By the time I reached the terminal, my focus was solely on giving passengers their best possible flight.

Regional flying brought its own special connections. Medical flights carrying patients to treatment, businesspeople closing crucial deals, families reuniting after months apart. Each flight profile demanded different skills: short hops required precise timing, longer sectors needed fuel management, but *all* required an understanding of the human cargo we carried.

In the cockpit between duties, I'd imagine the stories playing out behind me. *Who were they going to see? What adventures awaited? What chapters of their lives were unfolding at 30,000 feet?* Sometimes during cruise, watching the sun paint the clouds gold, I'd reflect on how many life-changing journeys I'd been part of.

Standing in the front galley during boarding, wearing those four stripes, something interesting often happened. People would share the most *intimate* details of their lives, as if my uniform granted some kind of confessional privilege.

'I haven't seen my parents for five years...'

'I've just had a miscarriage...'

'I'm meeting someone I've only known online for six months...'

'This is our first family holiday since my youngest was born...'

These weren't just 'passengers'; they were humans in transition, each flight marking a significant moment in their personal stories. The aircraft might have been full of strangers, but every seat held a unique person on a unique journey, and I had the privilege of being *part* of their story, even if only for a few hours.

Operating the aircraft satisfied my technical side, but these human connections fulfilled something deeper. Each flight represented hundreds of individual stories, and I had the privilege of playing a small part in all of them. Plus, I got to see sunshine every day.

What a wonderful privilege.

Losing My Virginity to Richard Branson

My time at Rex was invaluable—three years of solid experience that shaped me as a pilot. Like most regional airline pilots, I harboured bigger dreams.

When I started flying, my plan seemed crystal clear: Private licence first, then instructor rating, charter flying, Impulse Airlines, and finally the Holy Grail—Ansett. That was the pathway to joining those well-paid pilots with their enviable lifestyles.

Aviation has a way of rewriting your plans.

When Ansett went into receivership in 2001, the industry landscape shifted dramatically. Virgin Blue seized this opportunity, applying for their Air Operators Certificate to compete with Qantas. The timing was perfect—one giant had fallen, leaving room for a new player to reshape Australian aviation.

I'd experienced Virgin Blue's culture first-hand as a passenger. Being 28, tall and blonde probably didn't harm my chances of scoring jump seat rides for take-offs and landings. The crew were refreshingly different—their energy infectious. Smart uniforms, a joke book onboard, and a sense of fun that somehow made the pretty serious business of flying feel much more *human*.

The flight deck jump seat gave me a perfect view of their operation. Pilots maintained absolute professionalism while embracing the company's lighter side. Even the standard calls had a Virgin twist; but safety never took a back seat to style.

This chapter's title might have raised your eyebrows, suggesting a more scandalous path to Virgin employment. The reality was far more mundane. I applied online and my hours and experience as a Rex Captain secured the interview.

I had heard, through 'PPRuNe' (pilot rumour mill), about the specifics of the check test at Virgin Blue, so a friend and I went to Darling Harbour and hired the Flight Experience Simulator for 3 hours. Most people go to play; we went to learn.

After much negotiation with the junior pilot who worked at the simulator, Sarah and I were able to assume the Captain and First Officer seats (rather than him sitting next to us) and practised for 3 hours.

He had encouraged us to do what most tourists do, fly under the Sydney Harbour Bridge. Whilst iconic, this wouldn't help us preparing for the check scenarios we would experience at Virgin Blue.

Rex had given me the hours and experience I needed. Moving to Virgin Blue felt like the natural next step. What followed was 13 years with Virgin Blue and later rebranded to Virgin Australia—years that would see both the airline and myself transform in ways I never expected.

I had worked hard; it was good timing, and the Virgin Blue culture matched my own approach to aviation: professional, but never losing sight of the joy in flying.

Looking back, those carefully laid early career plans seem almost quaint. Aviation teaches you to be flexible, to recognise opportunities when they arise, and sometimes to throw away the map and chart a new course.

I did meet Sir Richard years later at a crew hotel in Sydney. He lived up to his reputation—engaging, warm, and genuinely interested in his crew's stories.

He even picked up the bar tab for everyone!

Part 7   Virgin First Officer

'Never interrupt someone doing something you said couldn't be done.' - Amelia Earhart

eMpTy

Fresh off passing my six-month probation as First Officer with Virgin Australia, I was rostered for a Sydney-Perth-Sydney rotation. The return leg was a 'Red-Eye'—one of those lovely overnight flights that really test your stamina. My probation reviews were thorough—everything from precise technical knowledge to crew resource management was under scrutiny. I'd earned my place in that right-hand seat, and with it came the responsibility to not only respect, but also *support*, my Captain's decisions.

My assigned Captain on this rotation had a reputation for being conservative with fuel. Not the *good* kind of conservative that keeps you safe, but the kind that cuts it close. He'd routinely take less than flight plan fuel if he could justify it. It never made *sense* to me—it wasn't coming out of his pay, and the small savings in fuel burn hardly seemed worth the reduced safety margin.

In Perth, preparing for our return flight, he announced his intention to take 500kg less fuel than the flight plan suggested, which was already a lean calculation, in my view. The flight plan was conservative, based on optimal conditions. Any deviation from *perfect* would eat into our reserves.

Studying the weather charts, I spotted a high-pressure system over Australia's east coast—perfect conditions for fog development over Sydney during our arrival time. Years of flying had taught me to read between the lines of weather forecasts—to *anticipate* conditions rather than just react to them.

I raised my concerns. 'You can tell by the synoptic chart there might be fog forming while we're enroute.'

'It's not on the flight plan, so we don't need it,' he dismissed.

'I disagree. The high-pressure system, clear skies, and light winds—it's textbook fog conditions. We won't have enough fuel if fog develops.'

'I am the Captain. It's my decision.'

Standing there at 10:30pm Perth time, I felt tears threatening. Nobody wants to be 'that' First Officer—the one who delays flights or causes problems. The aircraft was full, and my decision would affect everyone onboard, but years of training had taught me that popularity never trumps safety.

After a long moment, I packed my charts into my navigation bag and turned to the Captain. Despite my respect for his position and authority, I couldn't compromise on safety. 'I'm sorry, I can't continue knowing we don't have enough fuel to safely fly this flight.'

'You can leave then.'

I shook his hand. 'Goodnight.'

Walking off into the aerobridge, I was seriously wondering if I'd just ended my career. I called crewing. They connected me to the duty pilot—my Base Manager in Sydney.

I'd woken him up.

'What's wrong?' he asked.

'I've just offloaded myself from the flight,' I stated.

'What's up?'

I explained the situation and he said he would call me right back; he needed to get out of bed and become familiar with the flight details.

Five long minutes passed in that aerobridge, cabin crew staring, till he finally called back. He wanted more details. I explained the synoptic situation, our fuel reserves, and the likely fog development. After hearing both fuel calculations, he laughed and said he'd have taken even more than my suggested minimum of 1.5 tonnes extra.

'Get back on the plane.' he instructed.

'I can't, I've offloaded myself.'

'I'll call the Captain,' he said.

The Captain emerged minutes later. 'Get in.'

'Not until we have more reasonable fuel for the safety of the flight,' I stated.

'We'll go with your calculation then,' he conceded.

The flight was predictably awkward—just mandatory checklist calls and radio communications. Every routine check felt tense, every call strained. Then, 200 nautical miles from Sydney, the message I'd predicted: 'Hazard Alert. Sydney. Fog.'

The Captain wouldn't meet my eyes.

Our lighter tailwinds meant we'd burned more fuel than planned. Each calculation showed our margins shrinking. We had enough for one landing attempt in Sydney before diverting to Canberra. No margin for error. Even worse, traffic slowed us down on approach, burning precious fuel. Everything hinged on the Qantas 737 ahead of us making it through the fog. If they went around, we'd need to divert without even trying.

They landed. We followed.

After shutdown, not a word was exchanged between us. The paperwork was completed in silence; two professionals united only by procedure.

Years later, over beers during another overnight, that same Captain opened up to me about his controversial fuel decisions. He'd been hauled before the Chief Pilot for taking *too much* fuel. The company had been cracking down after discovering some pilots were adding extra tonnes just to 'stick it to' a former CEO they disliked—childish behaviour that increased fuel burn due to the additional weight.

After the company 'counselled' the main culprits, they'd formed a pact to take 'company fuel' or less—equally childish. Company fuel was the legal minimum calculated from weather forecasts, fuel burn averages, and published allowances for specific departure procedures. Some pilots, perhaps viewing it as a matter of control, would scrutinise every variable: requesting frequent weather updates to use more precise wind calculations, specifying exact departure routes rather than using standard figures—all to justify carrying even less fuel than the company's basic calculation.

While they'd never jeopardise safety, knowing they could always divert if needed, this approach turned routine flights into unnecessarily complex operations. The debate split the pilot group: those who wanted extra fuel to account for forecast inaccuracies and unexpected changes, versus those who argued that fewer fuel reserves actually simplified decision-making by limiting options. These more experienced pilots maintained that excess fuel could create an illusion of choice, potentially clouding critical decisions during deteriorating conditions. Yet finding the sweet spot between operational flexibility and financial efficiency remained an ongoing challenge—after all, every kilogram of extra fuel burned money.

The politics of fuel had transformed straightforward decisions into acts of rebellion or compliance. Eventually, the company revised its fuel policy to what this Captain had originally wanted, finding a middle ground that satisfied most pilots.

Understanding this history wouldn't have change my decision that night in Perth, however it highlighted how company culture, individual reactions, and operational decisions intertwine in aviation. I've always respected the authority and position of the Captain—it's fundamental to aviation safety. But respect should not extend to silent compliance when safety margins are at stake.

Standing your ground can mean standing alone. That night taught me that being right isn't always comfortable, but comfort isn't always safe. Speaking up wasn't just about protecting myself - it was about standing up for others who didn't feel able to.

I might be adventurous in life but never cavalier with anyone's safety. In aviation, the difference between conservative and cavalier can be measured in kilograms of fuel or, more importantly, in the courage to say 'No.'

Captain, Order Me a Tea, Please?

Male airline captains possess a peculiar magnetism. Whether it's their uniform or their status, they always attract attention—particularly from cabin crew, regardless of relationship status.

The transformation is remarkable: Invisible as First Officers; irresistible with that extra stripe on their epaulettes.

During another Red-Eye flight from Perth to Sydney, I witnessed this phenomenon firsthand. Our cabin supervisor entered the flight deck, ostensibly to take drink orders, but her true mission became immediately apparent.

Women recognise flirting in other women, even when the male recipients remain oblivious. This Captain was spectacularly unaware.

She wedged herself between our seats, back turned to me, laughing at his every mundane utterance. Each sentence earned a touch on his shoulder or arm. I'd seen this performance countless times, however tonight it was blocking my path to a simple cup of tea.

My requests for peppermint tea went unheard. She looked through me as if I were part of the aircraft's upholstery. Finally, I resorted to the intercom connecting me to the Captain's headset:

'Can you please order me a cup of tea?'

'Just ask her,' he suggested helpfully.

'I already have, twice! She's ignoring me.' He hadn't noticed, being understandably focused on flying the aircraft, and remained *equally* oblivious to 20 minutes of very determined flirtation that produced neither tea *nor* coffee.

Eventually, he mentioned we had work to do. She finally departed, leaving me to explain the obvious. 'She's into you.'

'No she's not. No one looks at me,' he replied with genuine bewilderment.

'When she returns, say something boring. If she laughs and touches your arm, she's interested.'

She delivered our drinks, my tea finally materialising.

'Top of descent is in an hour,' he stated, dry as Aviation Law regulations.

My suggested experiment had immediate success: his factual statement about top of descent earned a laugh and arm touch. His posture stiffened as realisation dawned.

'Thanks, we'll call you in half an hour, we're a bit busy right now,' he managed, suddenly fascinated by the instruments panel.

'Oh my god, what am I going to do with that?' he asked after she left.

'Nothing. You're married.'

The irony? Female captains rarely experience such attention. Like successful female comedians who intimidate potential partners while their male counterparts date supermodels, women in power face different dynamics. I knew a stunning First Officer whose dating prospects dried up the moment she earned her fourth stripe.

Watching newly promoted male captains adjust to their sudden allure provided endless entertainment. Colleagues who'd spent years lamenting their invisibility now found themselves bewildered by constant attention. Some handled it with grace, others stumbled through their newfound magnetism. One Captain confided he yearned for the simplicity of anonymity.

By the time I earned my fourth stripe, I'd developed a thorough understanding of flight deck sociology. The same crews who had looked through me as a First Officer now hung on my every preflight briefing. The technical content remained identical—only the audience's perception had shifted.

Experience on both sides of the epaulette stripe divide proved invaluable. Understanding a First Officer's hesitation to speak up, having lived it myself, shaped my command style. When junior crew raised concerns, they received the attention I'd once been denied.

The evolution of the aviation industry has been fascinating to witness. More women in command roles have gradually shifted perceptions, though old habits stubbornly persist. Female captains still get called "Dear" by ground staff who snap to attention for male counterparts. Male First Officers sometimes struggle with female command.

Yet aircraft respond to *competence,* not chromosomes. In critical moments, when split-second decisions matter, gender becomes irrelevant—proof that these social dynamics are learned, not innate. While professional boundaries between flight deck and cabin crew have been mostly clarified, human nature remains constant. You'll still witness the occasional starry-eyed crew member, and still observe the subtle blend of hierarchy with attraction.

Those early experiences of invisibility taught valuable lessons about leadership. While four stripes might command more attention than three, true authority stems from neither stripes nor gender, but from how you conduct yourself in the role.

I'm sure many captains of both sexes are more interested in their instrument panels than their adoring fans.

Dissent and Violating Safety

In commercial aviation, Cabin Supervisors represent more than their title suggests. Flight crew, including Captains and First Officers, respectfully refer to them as 'Cabin Captains'—a designation earned through their critical role in maintaining safety standards aboard our aircraft.

These professionals serve as our eyes and ears in the cabin, vital partners in ensuring passenger welfare and aircraft security. Those who violate safety procedures have no place in our operation, which explains the deep respect we hold for competent Cabin Captains.

My experience during a four-day rotation with Virgin Australia Regional Airlines (VARA) would test this relationship to its limits. Serving as First Officer alongside Captain Adam on a Perth route, our pre-flight experience proved unusual from the start.

The Perth-based cabin crew, including a Cabin Supervisor who had transferred from Sydney, scattered themselves across separate café tables rather than gathering as a unified crew, breaking from standard pre-flight protocol. Despite our attempts to establish rapport through greetings and smiles, their responses remained notably cold.

In aviation, pre-flight crew gatherings serve a vital purpose beyond mere socializing. These informal meetings, outside of formal briefings, allow crews to establish rapport, discuss potential concerns, and align on operational requirements. The crew's deliberate separation hinted at the challenges ahead.

The situation escalated at the aircraft. After racing ahead toward the boarding gate, the cabin crew chose the incorrect pathway, ignoring standard procedures that require flight crew to lead the way. Our aircraft had arrived as a 'dead ship'—unpowered and requiring complete start-up procedures and engineering checks.

While I attended to my pre-flight routine, including a necessary bathroom break before initiating the complex Auxiliary Power Unit (APU) start-up sequence, the Cabin Supervisor took an unprecedented step. She entered the flight deck without authorisation and activated both the APU and air conditioning systems—a serious breach of safety protocols.

'What are you doing?' I questioned, emerging from the bathroom to find her exiting the flight deck.

'Putting the air conditioning on,' she replied with casual indifference.

'Nothing was on.'

'That's OK. I know what to do. My boyfriend's a First Officer,' she stated, displaying unwarranted confidence.

'You're not allowed in the flight deck.'

Her response dripped with condescension: 'As I said, my boyfriend is a First Officer. I know what to do.'

This moment crystallized a dangerous misunderstanding of aviation hierarchy. The APU, essentially a small turbine engine in the aircraft's tail, requires specific start-up procedures to prevent electrical system damage and fire risks. Its initiation sequence demands careful timing: first starting the unit, then waiting for proper oil pressure and temperature stabilisation before adding electrical loads, and finally introducing air conditioning demand. Rushing this sequence risks catastrophic damage.

Captain Adam's response to this breach demonstrated exemplary leadership. Upon entering the flight deck and learning of the unauthorised access, he called her back.

'Did you do this?' he questioned directly.

'As I said to Michelle, I know what to do. My boyfriend is a First Officer,' she responded, rolling her eyes.

'Are you employed as a Pilot in Virgin?'

'No.'

'Well, we are now going to have to get an engineer to check this aircraft, because in effect you have grounded this aircraft,' Adam explained professionally.

'Don't be so melodramatic,' came her exasperated response.

I couldn't believe what I was hearing. The belligerence was extraordinary.

'Ok, we are shutting the aircraft down. You will have to do all your checks again,' he explained.

We didn't know what else she had touched, and safety was paramount.

The engineer's inspection, though relatively quick, highlighted the seriousness of unauthorised system access. Each check represented time spent ensuring passenger safety hadn't been compromised by well-intentioned but *dangerous* interference.

Our FIFO (Fly-In-Fly-Out) charter flight to Boolgeeda that day revealed further safety violations. Throughout the flight, the crew failed to maintain mandatory 20-minute check-ins with the flight deck. These check-ins are not mere formality—they ensure cabin security, monitor passenger welfare, and maintain crew situational awareness throughout the flight.

Flying into Boolgeeda offers pilots a spectacular introduction to the Pilbara's ancient landscape. The massive impact crater, formed millions of years ago, creates distinctive weather patterns and requires specific considerations to the aircraft's approach. Its rim rises dramatically from the rust-red earth, spanning several kilometres—a testament to the immense forces that shaped this region. For pilots, this geological formation affects wind patterns and thermal activity, demanding careful attention during approach and landing phases.

The mining operations that necessitate these FIFO flights have transformed this remote location into a crucial hub for Australia's resources sector. Despite regular service, each approach demands meticulous attention to detail, regardless of crew familiarity with the route.

Post-landing procedures require a mandatory three-minute engine cool-down period—a manufacturer-specified requirement adopted globally. Despite clear briefing on this procedure, due to a shorter than normal taxi time to the bay, the crew committed their most serious breach: opening the aft (rear) door while engines remained running. This triggered a master caution light in the flight deck, necessitating immediate engine shutdown to prevent potential hazards.

The crew's response proved even more concerning than the breach itself. When the Captain investigated, he encountered outright denial.

'What was the problem in the back?' he asked.

'There was no problem,' the Supervisor replied.

'We got an indication in the flight deck that the door was open whilst the engines were still running.'

'No, it wasn't,' she claimed.

This back-and-forth continued until the Captain stated firmly, 'OK. We can do this back and forth all day. We know what we saw. You don't have that indicator in the cabin. Who are the two cabin crew down the back, we need to talk to them.'

'We don't have time for that,' she responded.

'You don't understand,' said the Captain, 'if there is a fault, then we can't go.'

She called her two colleagues from the back of the plane to come up.

Adam asked them, 'Who was sitting closest to the door?'

His response was surly as he looked at Adam and said, 'That was me.'

Adam asked him what happened, and explained a light came on indicating the door had been opened while the engines were still running.

'No, it hadn't,' stated the male cabin crew member, with a tone of voice indicating that neither Adam, nor myself, really knew what we were talking about.

I was due to do a walk around of the plane before the return flight, however I asked Adam if I could stay and hear the conversation. I wanted to know how he would handle this clear dissent. This was part of my learning on the job—seeing how an experienced captain would handle his crew being disrespectful and bordering on belligerent. It was also quite entertaining to see how *brazen* they were in defying the Captain. I'd never seen anything like this before in my aviation career.

Adam said, 'Again, we can keep going over this, but an indicator light came on telling us the rear door was opened whilst the engines were still on.'

We have a mode control panel on the 737 where indicator lights appear. Adam pointed to it, and pushed the annunciator warning button to show it was in working order.

He pointed to where the light came on and said, 'No other light came on. Just the one that tells us the rear door was opened whilst the engines were still going.'

'No, no, the engines were stopped,' he retorted.

'It doesn't come on as a warning light if the engines have been shut down. It will only come on if the engines are still running.'

They continued to argue with Adam, so he said, 'We need to get an engineer to check the plane. I hope you brought an overnight bag because they must be flown from Broome to Boolgeeda. We will probably have to stay here overnight. Start securing the aircraft.'

They now looked very sheepish and went away.

'You know they opened the door,' I said to Adam.

'I know. I want to see how long it takes,' he replied.

We didn't call the engineer.

They eventually came back to the flight deck. We were making a bit of a show about packing up the flight deck. Adam told the ground staff to hold off boarding the new passengers.

The cabin supervisor and the crew member from the back of the plane stood there and eventually he said, 'I thought the seatbelt sign went off, so I opened the door.' He had changed his tone.

'We didn't do the seatbelt sign,' we told him.

'I was sure I heard the seatbelt sign, and then I opened the door,' he replied.

'So, you did open the door whilst the engine was still going?' Adam asked.

'I'm not saying that! I'm saying I heard the seatbelt sign go off, and then I opened the door,' he defended.

'Unless you tell me that you opened the door, whilst the engines were going, we have a fault with the aircraft and we can't go,' Adam stated calmly.

The crew member walked away, and eventually came back to say, 'I opened the door whilst the engines were going because I thought I heard the seatbelt sign go off.'

'OK. Let's get the aircraft ready. Get the passengers on, and we can deal with this back in Perth.'

The return flight proceeded in tense silence, with the crew withdrawing all communication and service, extending *beyond* discourtesy to potential safety concerns. Upon landing, they abandoned their end-of-flight duties, leaving bins unemptied and safety equipment unsecured before rushing to file a complaint alleging bullying from the flight deck.

The implications of this incident reverberated throughout regional operations. It prompted a comprehensive review of crew training protocols, particularly regarding flight deck access and ground procedures. The airline strengthened its emphasis on crew resource management training, using this incident as a case study in how seemingly minor procedural breaches can escalate into significant safety concerns.

The aftermath served as a stark reminder of aviation's uncompromising approach to safety. The Cabin Supervisor lost her position, while the crew member responsible for the door incident resigned shortly after.

Their departures reinforced a fundamental aviation truth: safety procedures aren't mere *suggestions,* and experience in adjacent roles doesn't qualify one to override established protocols.

Industry-wide, similar incidents have led to the development of more robust safety management systems. These systems now place greater emphasis on crew dynamics and the importance of maintaining professional boundaries, regardless of personal relationships or previous experience.

The incident also highlighted the critical role of proper reporting procedures and the need for clear documentation of safety breaches.

In aviation, each protocol exists as the culmination of lessons learned through experience, often at great cost. The dismissal of these procedures, regardless of intent or assumed knowledge, undermines the robust safety culture that defines modern commercial aviation.

This incident stands as a powerful reminder that maintaining safety standards requires *constant* vigilance, clear communication, and unwavering adherence to those established protocols.

The implications of this incident extended beyond immediate operational concerns. It highlighted the importance of proper crew selection, ongoing training, and the maintenance of professional standards throughout all levels of airline operations. In an industry where safety margins leave no room for compromise, the importance of following established procedures *cannot* be overstated.

Flying showed me how much teamwork matters. Clear rules and working well together keep everyone safe, especially when things don't go as planned.

Ladies of the Flight

Flying FIFO routes out of Perth to remote locations like Port Hedland, Karratha, and Boolgeeda, meant regular encounters with mining workers, in their high-visibility clothing and dusty work boots. Among these passengers, a distinct group stood out—well-dressed ladies heading to these remote mining towns.

During flights, conversations revealed many were 'friends', or 'cousins' of other passengers. Some claimed to be hairdressers. I guess that even mining workers need their haircut regularly.

The mining industry's demographics created an interesting dynamic: workers stationed in remote locations, spending extended periods away from civilisation, sought companionship. Physical affection and 'special cuddles' became a commodity, particularly appealing to single workers with limited recreational options in these isolated mining communities.

The contrast between fluorescent workwear and elegant attire told its own story of supply meeting demand in Australia's remote mining towns.

Cat in The Overhead Locker

This is childish. I am acknowledging this!
Late-night flights from Bali could stretch into monotonous hours. With sleeping passengers, minimal cabin crew activity, and quiet radios, pilots occasionally sought harmless entertainment. One particular Captain broke the silence by making barely audible meowing sounds over the PA system.

We shared a laugh and returned to our duties, considering it a momentary diversion.

Later, the cabin crew reported passengers opening the overhead lockers, searching for a phantom cat.

Unbeknownst to us, our simple prank had sparked a full-scale feline investigation throughout the aircraft. As dawn rose during our descent into Sydney, the Captain couldn't resist one final meow. The cabin crew's immediate response confirmed our passengers remained committed to their search.

'Did you hear that?' came the question, 'There is a meow. Passengers are wondering where the cat is?' He responded in the negative.

No cat was ever found, nor harmed in this childish prank. We never spoke of or repeated it again.

Lady MacGyver

Left Over In A Hotel

Pilots develop flight-route fatigue, particularly regarding repetitive meal options—Thai chicken curry somehow loses its appeal after 200+ servings. This situation spawned an urban legend, supported by alleged photographic evidence, of desperate late-night foraging by hungry aviators.

Picture a familiar hotel corridor, traversed countless times by weary pilots. Late arrivals often find room service closed, with exhaustion ruling out venturing into the city.

You need *food*.

The corridors become hunting grounds for sustenance. Vending machines prove rare in these upscale establishments, leading to more creative, less classy solutions.

In the distance: abandoned room service trays, their contents beckoning. These flat receptacles of nourishment, discarded adjacent to rooms containing now-sleeping inhabitants, offer very tempting possibilities. The corridors become silent stages for stealthy midnight raids, as pilots move from floor to floor, seeking sustenance.

One Captain's midnight hunting expedition became legendary among crew members. His adventure, possibly documented in photographic evidence that still circulates, sparked both amusement and contemplation among fellow pilots. His subsequent challenge to 'give it a try' echoed in my mind during my own moments of desperate hunger in countless hotel corridors.

I may have been encouraged—no, *challenged*—to attempt it myself during particularly famished nights.

Though I've *considered* it during moments of quiet, hungry desperation, I've left such culinary adventures to more intrepid souls.

SAM

Society affords certain professionals automatic respect—doctors and airline captains among them. Before earning my captain's stripes, I placed pilots on a pedestal. Upon achieving that rank, reality struck; captains remained human, complete with frailties and faults. The moment you turn left into the cockpit, you're still simply a *person*. While the flight deck houses many remarkable individuals, some struggle with personal challenges that overwhelm their professional demeanour.

Captain SAM—Small Angry Man—cast a long shadow over our airline. His reputation for intimidation preceded him, causing FOs to feign illness rather than share his cockpit. Crewing staff withheld his identity during draft calls, knowing volunteers would vanish at his mention.

My first encounter proved confronting. During our initial flight, as we approached for landing, I noticed his hand hovering unnervingly close to mine on the controls, exceeding standard safety protocols. This intrusive oversight suggested to me distrust rather than readiness to assist in an emergency. When I saw his hand over mine, I immediately thought I had missed something critical.

Nervously I asked what was wrong. He ignored the query, and I continued on to a standard, uneventful landing. His tension only eased once he controlled our taxi to the bay.

This hovering continued through subsequent flights, transforming routine operations into ordeals. When my frustration finally peaked, I was very close to shouting, 'Then you fly it!' as many other pilots had done.

The experience contradicted everything I'd learned as a flying instructor, where we encouraged students to take control early to build confidence. We allowed them to make mistakes and guided them towards solutions—a crucial part of the learning process. Errors under supervision create valuable teaching moments, far preferable to mistakes made alone in the air.

Instruction requires confidence in one's own abilities. Self-doubt would only impede student progress. To maintain our own assurance, we regularly flew with more experienced instructors, expanding our own comfort zones through continued learning.

Initially, I avoided flights with SAM, when possible. However, as time passed, the tension became unsustainable. Something needed to *change*. During a Perth flight—5.5 hours of cruise time, I gently but directly confronted him about his overbearing presence. The lengthy flight provided ample opportunity to address our difficult dynamic.

SAM revealed that two near-catastrophic incidents with previous First Officers had spawned his perpetual mistrust. These experiences had scarred him deeply, leading to his hypervigilant approach to supervision. He claimed to relax once pilots proved their competence, though this process could span months or years.

While I disagreed with his methods, I *understood* the challenge, to earn the trust of a colleague deeply scarred by past experiences. I also gained insight into the man when he opened up to me; he became less intimidating.

Each flight became a trial, a test of my skills and patience. Success required maintaining professionalism while demonstrating competence under his scrutiny.

The irregular nature of pilot pairings meant building his trust took years rather than months. Progress came slowly through consistent performance and unwavering professionalism.

The breakthrough finally arrived during a challenging Sydney approach, fighting blustery westerly winds. The conditions demanded precision and confidence, heightened by SAM's presence. To my surprise, he remained relaxed in his seat as I managed the demanding landing.

Years of demonstration had finally earned his trust. The satisfaction and pride in that moment transformed the atmosphere of our cockpit. Looking back, perhaps the change indicated more about his growing confidence than my proven capabilities. The experience taught me valuable lessons about patience, persistence, and the complex dynamics of professional relationships in aviation.

Human Factors

Pilots and surgeons share crucial personality traits—both require exceptional focus and motor control while performing critical tasks. When a surgeon operates, you want their complete attention on the next incision, not nervously contemplating the human beneath their hands. Similarly, pilots must maintain calm under pressure, focusing solely on their immediate tasks.

However, this level of perfectionism presents unique challenges. Research shows it strongly correlates with higher markers of narcissism.

To help pilots check their God complex at the door, our airline implemented Human Factors training, designed to increase emotional intelligence and improve cockpit–cabin dynamics. When expressions of interest circulated for instructors, I immediately volunteered. Teaching had always deepened my understanding of subjects, and human behaviour fascinates me.

The course had two components. The pilots attending morning sessions were focusing on incident analysis and human error contributions; while afternoon sessions combined pilots with cabin crew for broader discussions. A dedicated Cabin Crew Facilitator co-led these joint sessions, bringing valuable perspectives from the cabin environment.

During one particularly memorable afternoon session, when the cabin crew joined us after lunch, a female crew member casually extracted nail polish from her handbag and began painting her nails.

The tension in the classroom mounted as participants—experienced pilots and cabin crew—watched intently. Many had faced similar situations where minor infractions challenged authority. Their eyes conveyed a clear message: this disruption, though seemingly trivial, represented a test of leadership.

Senior captains, who regularly managed complex crew dynamics, observed with particular interest. They understood that small challenges to authority, if left unchecked, could evolve into larger safety concerns.

The smell of nail polish filled the room as the silence grew, an unspoken pressure existed to maintain professional standards.

Initially, I considered letting it slide, however the chemical smell started distracting other participants. They looked expectantly between me and my co-facilitator, waiting to see who would address the situation.

While my colleague continued teaching, I knelt beside the nail painter, and whispered a request to put the nail polish away. Though quiet, my intervention drew everyone's attention.

'No. I'm going out tonight and I *have* to do my nails,' she announced loudly, dismissing my request.

'Can you just put it away till after the lesson? Or do it in the break?' I suggested reasonably.

With exaggerated exasperation, as if explaining something obvious to a child, she repeated, 'No. I'm going *out!*'

By now, my co-facilitator had stopped teaching, and all eyes focused on the unfolding situation. The class watched the exchange with increasing interest—would this challenge to authority simply go unaddressed?

'Can we please have a chat out in the hallway?' I asked, attempting to maintain my professional composure despite her escalating defiance.

In the corridor, I tried again, 'Why do you need to do this during the class?'

'Because I am going out,' she repeated, rolling her eyes dramatically.

'You're at work now and you need to learn this. Can it wait?'

'I'm listening,' she insisted, though her attention clearly lay elsewhere.

'The smell is distracting others. Would you please wait until after class?'

'I Don't Think You Understand,' she emphasised each word. 'I'm going out after this, and I need it to dry.'

Seeking compromise, I suggested, 'Why don't you bring your polish and do it out here?'

Her face lit up in unexpected victory, 'Really?'

She grabbed her supplies and continued her manicure in the hallway while we resumed teaching.

The incident had perfectly illustrated the human factors we discussed in class—how personal priorities shouldn't override professional responsibilities, and also how different personality types approach conflict resolution.

Later, several pilots commented that the incident exemplified why Human Factors training proved essential. The simple act of painting nails had revealed complex dynamics in terms of authority, respect, and professional boundaries. The class's reaction demonstrated how even minor disruptions could impact team dynamics and test leadership responses.

The cabin crew underwent testing on the theoretical components of the workshop, with additional crew-specific training following the pilot's departure. Given her absence during crucial content, my co-facilitator marked her as absent from the course—a decision that highlighted the importance of professional conduct and full participation in safety training.

The incident itself became a teaching moment, demonstrating how personality traits, priorities, and perception all influence workplace interactions. It reinforced why Human Factors training proves to be essential in aviation—where teamwork, communication, and mutual respect directly impact safety outcomes.

UFO or UAV?

I used to get asked, a lot: Do you ever see anything whilst flying that is out of the ordinary? Do you believe in UFOs? Was the earth flat? Do you spray chemtrails whilst flying? I occasionally joked about earning extra pay for operating the chemtrail switch—after carefully donning our gas masks.

These 'chemtrails', known as contrails, stretching across the sky have a simple scientific explanation. They form when warm air meets cool, moist conditions—specifically when cool air enters a hot aircraft engine, then exits as hot, moist air into the cold atmosphere. Wing tip vortices curling behind aircraft wings demonstrate this principle—warm air from friction, meeting humid environment, creates visible swirls. Despite the conspiracy theories, that explanation remains purely scientific.

An incident on a night flight from Brisbane to Sydney defied any easy explanation. I was on a curfew chaser. The last flight into Sydney for the evening. We had been dodging storms all day so were racing to get back in time. At cruise altitude, we spotted a distant light above us.

Pilots share an international greeting ritual: flicking landing or wingtip lights signals recognition of passing aircraft. We assumed the light up above was another aircraft passing us overhead. We were at 40,000 ft so perhaps military or a private jet capable of reaching 53,000 feet... though our radar showed nothing.

The light began dancing erratically, making sharp directional changes. Goosebumps rose on my arms. Neither of us in the cockpit spoke, watching with widened eyes. After passing it, we exchanged looks of disbelief, our silence unbroken.

Other aircraft voices crackled over the radio, 'Did you see that? My goodness, did you see that?'

Air traffic control's response proved equally mysterious—they claimed ignorance of any unusual activity. The incident remains unexplained, leaving me to wonder: Did we witness a genuine UFO?

The question lingers, unanswered.

What a Bitch

During a turnaround, with passengers disembarked and the aircraft cleaned, we had 90 minutes before the next boarding.

While the crew headed to the terminal for a coffee, I remained with the aircraft to conduct my walkaround inspection: a routine check of the aircraft's external components for safety and operational integrity.

It didn't take long to complete the walkaround and I entered the plane via the rear stairs. Nothing could have prepared me for what I encountered. Two cabin crew had seized their brief downtime for an intimate encounter in the rear galley, their trousers around their ankles. Though I'm not prudish, witnessing such behaviour in our workplace left me stunned—a place we conducted safety briefings and prepared passenger services had become their private rendezvous spot!

Standing in shocked silence as they hastily dressed, I finally managed, 'What the F%ck?'

'Don't say anything,' he demanded.

'What the *actual* F%ck?' I expanded, still processing the scene.

Walking up the aisle, struggling to comprehend what I'd witnessed, a touch on my shoulder stopped me. As I turned, he pleaded, '*Please* don't say anything?'

His partner interjected with, 'Don't be a bitch.'

'I haven't decided on what I am going to do, but calling me a bitch isn't doing you any favours,' I stated firmly.

As I walked away toward the flight deck, 'bitch' echoed behind me a second time.

Turning back, I asked, 'Seriously?'

One offender opted to call in sick for the next sector, while the other continued the flight.

Their behaviour violated *multiple* company policies and countless professional standards. Though I could have—and perhaps *should* have—reported the incident, I chose discretion.

However, their defensive attitudes and hostile name-calling, rather than professional contrition, made their conduct even more egregious.

Still, their parting words lingered—F%ck you Bitch, indeed.

Lady MacGyver

I Would Look Better in That Uniform

Frank Sinatra's sultry voice crescendos, 'Come fly with me, let's fly, let's fly away,' Pretty young things emerge from buildings, ride Sydney ferries, drive convertibles. 'If you can use, some exotic booze, there's a bar in far Bombay. Come fly with me, let's fly, lets fly away!' Cue trumpets.

As Virgin Australia's token female pilot at the time, media engagements and promotional work frequently landed on my schedule. Frank's iconic song backed a major Virgin Australia advertising campaign, taking me to Eastern Creek motorway for filming. The location provided the perfect backdrop for superimposing aircraft imagery.

The shoot utilised a (real) Virgin Captain, engineer, and cabin crew member, and numerous extras. After hair and make-up, we walked the motorway repeatedly, perfecting timing and smiles while cameras captured various angles.

Between takes, a strikingly handsome man approached—chiselled jaw, perfect hair, model-worthy features. He surveyed me critically, hands on hips, then asked, 'How did YOU get to be the pilot? I'd look so much better in that uniform than you.'

'You probably would,' I agreed, 'but I am an actual pilot.'

He took his gorgeous face away and walked off.

Come fly with me, let's fly, let's fly away!

Twins and Wheels

My pregnancy coincided with my friend and fellow pilot, Captain Carol. I saw her as a mentor, and we had a lot of fun flying together. Her pregnancy was about a month further along than mine, but as I was having twins, we looked equally expectant around the waist.

During one of our final flights before pregnancy grounding, we flew together—Carol as Captain, me as First Officer. These last flights held special significance, marking the temporary end of our flying careers due to aviation's strict pregnancy regulations.

Approaching the departure lounge together, we silently coordinated an impromptu performance. Exaggerating our pregnant postures, hands supporting our lower backs, we waddled past concerned passengers toward the gate and down the aerobridge. Internal laughter bubbled as we imagined their reactions to two heavily pregnant pilots. The passengers' worried glances and whispered conversations only fuelled our amusement.

During the flight, a message reached the flight deck requesting that if either pregnant pilots went into labour, could we kindly delay until after landing. The cabin crew's deadpan delivery of this message made it even more entertaining.

Earlier in my pregnancy, morning sickness struck during a pre-flight walkaround.

Unlike the occasional vomiting during my early flying training years, pregnancy nausea proved unpredictable. Reaching the second wheel, nausea overwhelmed me. After confirming no observers in the vicinity, I discreetly vomited at the tyre's base. Intending to clean up with bottled water, I completed my inspection, chatted with an engineer and baggage handler, then *completely* forgot my intended cleaning duty.

During pushback, the engineer's voice crackled over the radio, 'Who did the walkaround?'

'I did,' I replied.

'Did you notice anything wrong with the aircraft?' he questioned.

'No.'

'There happened to be vomit on one of the wheels. Know anything about that?' he asked.

My face flushed crimson as I apologised profusely. The evidence of my morning sickness remained for all ground crew to see.

My Captain turned it into a running joke, ribbing me on every subsequent walkaround, asking if I needed a wheel for sickness. His good natured teasing followed me through my remaining flight duties. Thankfully, the incident remained singular, though it added another colourful chapter to the unique challenges of being a pregnant pilot.

Cancerous Interruptus

At 20 weeks pregnant with twins, aviation regulations grounded my flying career. This rule extends beyond pilots to *all* pregnant passengers—after 30 weeks, airlines require medical clearance letters confirming fitness to fly. Babies being born on board is bad for business. (I'm loving the alliteration in that last sentence!)

My obstetrician strongly recommended *earlier* grounding, citing the additional stresses of twins. The airline demonstrated exceptional support, accommodating me with ground duties. As my pregnancy advanced, they transitioned me to home-based work auditing pilot medicals—essentially data entry, however it maintained my vital connection to the pilot community. Working in pyjamas proved increasingly necessary as my body adapted to carrying twins, though I missed the skies desperately.

My twins were born slightly early at 35 weeks, a common timeline for multiple births. My son, born second, faced immediate complications requiring intensive neonatal care at a different hospital. The separation from my newborn tore at my heart while I recovered with my daughter. Every beeping monitor in my ward reminded me of my son's absence.

After persistent advocacy—more accurately, relentless maternal *determination*—my daughter and I transferred to join him. Every moment apart had felt like an eternity, but his condition improved rapidly once reunited.

Home life with twins introduced a bone-deep exhaustion I'd never known, accompanied by waves of postpartum blues that crashed against my usually resilient spirit. Long walks with the double stroller became my lifeline, my feet pounding the pavement in attempts to walk away from the overwhelming emotions. In retrospect, I was likely trying to outpace postpartum depression, one step at a time.

The physical demands of caring for twins, while managing my own recovery, tested my every reserve.

During precious nap times, I immersed myself in aviation studies, wistfully preparing for my eventual return to the skies. Videos about the 737 became my background noise, company policies my bedtime reading, procedures and operating limitations my constant companions. The return to flying loomed with a mountain of requirements: written exams, simulator sessions, check flights, and intensive line training with a check Captain before full reinstatement.

Each step represented another layer of separation from my babies yet also promised a return to the career I loved.

Those early months blur together in memory—endless cycles of feeding, changing, soothing, and stolen moments of study. Sleep deprivation coloured everything, making simple tasks feel monumental. Yet determination drove me forward. My older child needed attention too, so there was a constant balancing act of infant care with my older son, ensuring he didn't feel displaced by his new siblings.

Returning to work unleashed tsunamis of maternal guilt. Each departure felt like abandonment, though rationally I knew better. Yet work provided unexpected sanctuary from the relentless cycle of parenting duties.

Simple pleasures, like uninterrupted hotel room showers, felt decadently luxurious. These breaks recharged my depleted batteries, allowing me to return home at 100% for my children, somewhat alleviating the constant remorse.

Nearing my final check flight, during a rare peaceful overnight stay, I indulged in a bath instead of my usual rushed shower. At 16, my mother had instilled the crucial habit of regular breast self-checks. *The Women's Weekly* magazine's shower card, permanently fixed over our shower head, guided our examinations during those three minutes often while the conditioner did its work. This simple ritual had become second nature, until my recent motherhood relegated self-care to rushed showers, always with one eye on the twins lying on the bathroom floor.

That hotel bath, finally allowing proper time for relaxation and self-examination, revealed something concerning—a lump along my bra line. Though breastfeeding typically caused lumps and tenderness, something felt different. Warm water massage didn't dissipate it. The following night's shower confirmed its persistent presence, unmoved and unchanged. Fear crept in, but professional focus pushed it aside temporarily.

The timing couldn't have been worse with my flight check approaching. I compartmentalised, focusing solely on passing my return-to-work Check Flight.

After succeeding, I resumed flying with a Captain I particularly enjoyed working with. During another overnight stay, examining the lump again confirmed my growing fears. Its texture resembled wet cotton wool rubbed between fingers—neither typically spongy nor pellet-hard, but distinctly *wrong*.

I saw my doctor the next day.

The biopsy procedure followed swiftly; results promised within days. During another Brisbane overnight, the doctor called requesting an immediate office visit. I explained my travel schedule, requesting phone results.

'No, just enjoy your holiday, and come in when you get back to Sydney,' she reassured, her forced cheerfulness setting off internal alarms.

'Is there anything to worry about?' I enquired.

'I don't want to discuss anything on the phone. Just come see me when you return,' she said.

Anxiety snowballed during the next sector. I confided in my Captain as we headed to Melbourne, then Sydney, then back to Brisbane for the night.

In Melbourne, discussing my situation with the line manager triggered unexpected emotions. My mind was shadow-boxing with all the bad potentials. He started to get a little teary, hearing my predicament, which made *me* start to get teary, and then I started to cry. His sister's recent Stage 4 diagnosis struck too close to home. Tears flowed freely, professional composure crumbling under the weight of uncertainty.

He deemed me emotionally unfit to fly—a decision I couldn't dispute. After regaining composure, with the other Captain's agreement, I continued to Sydney, my duty ending there.

'When we land, you be the *first* one off, and then get to the doctor,' my Captain instructed.

The race to my doctor's office proved futile—she'd left minutes before. The next morning's appointment was with my mother's steady presence. We entered the doctor's office who then immediately started to cry. My mum and I looked at each other as this confirmed our fears. Cancer. Immediate treatment would begin.

A private breast cancer specialist near home offered hope, however protocol required initial consultation at Westmead Public Hospital's breast cancer unit. The cramped, understaffed facility, buried in the hospital's depths, without even mobile reception, served as a sobering introduction to my new reality. Patients and partners—both men and women facing breast cancer—waited hours reading outdated magazines, each lost in private battles with their circumstances.

The wait stretched endlessly. Every face in that room told a story of interrupted lives, of plans derailed, of futures suddenly uncertain. Some partners held hands tightly; others sat in hollow silence. The lack of mobile reception forced everyone to sit with their thoughts—no escape into digital distraction.

Treatment options included lumpectomy, radiation, or mastectomy. Given my age and potential future pregnancies, they advised against mastectomy. However, my small breasts had never defined my femininity or self-image. With three young children depending on me, eradicating every trace of cancer became my sole priority. Their futures outweighed any attachment I had to my physical form.

They disagreed, but I got my way.

Post-mastectomy chemotherapy posed another crossroad.

Despite my alternative therapy upbringing and my social circle's holistic preferences, I embraced Western medicine's full arsenal. Complementary therapies served alongside, helping manage side effects, however I wanted *every* possible weapon in my fight. Complete hair loss followed—save one stubborn eyelash that still warranted its daily mascara, my small act of defiance against the disease.

I bought a wig, but the twins freaked out, so I pivoted to hats.

Aviation regulations required a cancer diagnosis report to CASA within seven days, triggering immediate medical suspension. My adventures in the sky entered an indefinite holding pattern. Fortunately, accrued sick leave and a remarkable company donation program provided two years' salary coverage before insurance became necessary—a safety net that allowed focus on healing rather than finances.

I've heard the pilot sick leave donation scheme no longer exists; very unfortunate.

The twins kept me grounded in more ways than one. Their constant needs left little time for self-pity, though nights brought darker thoughts. My older child understood something was wrong but couldn't grasp why Mummy's hair disappeared or why she seemed so tired. His confusion mirrored my own struggle to comprehend this new reality.

After six months leave, I returned 30 days post my last chemotherapy session—likely prematurely, given the lingering fatigue that permeated every cell. Chemo-induced menopause brought unexpected challenges: hot flashes during critical flight phases, brain fog during complex calculations. Thankfully, it hadn't been that long since the training I'd completed after maternity leave, so I still had all my notes.

Looking back, I really should have taken more time off to build up my strength and take some time out for *me*.

The company's support extended to CEO-approved permission to wear a head scarf during recovery, acknowledging both practical and emotional needs during this transition.

My first return to the flight deck brought both anxiety and relief. The familiar environment of the cockpit offered comfort, yet everything felt slightly altered through the lens of survival. One training Captain's comment on my scarf broke the tension, 'What are you wearing that for? You look ridiculous! You look like a pirate.' After explaining my situation, his attitude changed.

'Don't be silly. Take it off. I don't care what you look like.'

I removed it. His quick double-take and immediate response to 'Put it back on!' sparked my genuine laughter, a precious moment of normalcy in an otherwise altered reality.

When my hair *finally* started to grow back, it emerged with a mind of its own—curly and unruly, decidedly *pubic-like* in texture. Bleach transformed it into a blonde afro, a look I chose to embrace fully—a pale Diana Ross, minus her voice, looks, and talent! Learning to laugh at these changes helped heal more than just my body, for besides my hair falling out, my marriage was falling apart.

This harrowing experience ultimately sparked positive change. Writing to CEO John Borghetti about my mother's shower card influence, I proposed similar employee outreach. The company partnered with the Breast Cancer Foundation, distributing shower cards to all 1,800 pilots and thousands of additional employees. I'd like to think that perhaps my journey through darkness helped guide others toward early detection through self-examination. They were mailed out in privacy.

Cancer changed more than my body—it altered my perspective on life, death, and the precious time in between. Each flight now carries additional meaning, each moment with my children holds deeper significance. The scars tell a story not of loss, but of survival, resilience, and the power of early detection.

In sharing this story, I hope to remind others that even in our *busiest* moments, self-care isn't selfish—it's downright essential.

Sometimes, three minutes examining yourself with hair conditioner can make the difference between life and death.

The twins are older now, likely unaware of how their early months intertwined with this battle, yet their presence during that time provided purpose and joy amid much darkness. Every milestone they reach reminds me why the fight mattered *so* much. We all survived—changed, strengthened, and more grateful for each day we share together.

Female Baton

Three years after my cancer treatment, the Australian Women Pilots' Association (AWPA) launched an initiative that celebrated the strength and spirit of women in aviation. Female pilots across the country united to inspire the next generation of aviators while supporting a cause close to my heart.

The Women Pilots' Relay Fundraiser began at Victoria's Avalon Air Show. A commemorative baton would journey 28,000 kilometres around Australia, passing through the hands of 72 female pilots, each flight raising money for cancer research through passenger donations and corporate contributions.

AWPA President, Captain Carol, approached Virgin Australia with an ambitious proposal: schedule an all-female crew flight as part of the relay. The airline embraced the initiative, rostering Carol and I to fly together from Darwin to Perth. They donated ticket proceeds and permitted passenger donation announcements during the flight.

The public's response proved overwhelming. As the baton passed from Captain Carol's hands to mine, then onward to another female colleague in Perth, tears welled in our eyes. This wasn't just about raising funds—it celebrated women in aviation while supporting a cause that had touched so many lives.

During our sector, passengers shared deeply personal stories of their own cancer battles or loved ones lost. Their generous donations were accompanied by tears, hugs, and a profound connection that transformed our flight into something far more meaningful than a simple journey from Darwin to Perth.

As the baton continued its journey around Australia, it carried with it not just our signatures, but the hopes, struggles, and triumphs of everyone touched by this disease.

Another Empty Kitchen

Female pilots make up merely 6% of all pilots worldwide. Male colleagues would often mutter 'another empty kitchen' when they spotted us in operations or walking through terminals. The jab stung, carrying centuries of prejudice in four simple words.

We developed our own response. When Captain, First Officer, and cabin crew were all female, we proudly called it an 'unmanned flight.' The term caught on, with some male pilots playfully dubbing their all-male crews 'manned flights'.

At Virgin, the numbers painted a stark picture. Among 1800 pilots, only 41 were female, with only 11 holding Captain stripes. These demographics created a natural sisterhood. Between flights, we gathered in quiet corners of crew rooms, sharing advice about tricky approaches, swapping stories of overcoming doubts, celebrating promotions.

The senior female captains became treasured mentors, teaching us to navigate both complex weather patterns *and* workplace politics with equal grace and skill.

One female Captain had grown from being a colleague to a close friend. We shared meals, stories, dreams beyond the flight deck. I introduced her to my mum, a skilled kinesiologist, who helped her through some emotional and physical struggles. Our friendship deepened when I drove her to, and supported her through, an abortion, despite being pregnant with my twins at the time. That day created a bond I thought unbreakable.

During maternity leave though our connection had frayed. Messages went unanswered, calls unreturned. She'd had relationship troubles, then started dating again. I reached out regularly, worried about her wellbeing, blaming her silence on life's chaos rather than seeing the warning signs.

Throughout my cancer journey, the other female pilots rallied around me, bringing meals, offering rides to treatment, keeping my aviation skills sharp through technical discussions during recovery. Their support proved invaluable.

Three months after finally returning to the flight deck, Crewing called with a last-minute opportunity. A draft. Extra pay for filling an empty slot. My heart lifted when they mentioned her name as Captain. Two years had passed. This four-sector day promised time to perhaps rebuild our friendship.

Hamilton Island presented unique challenges that demanded careful planning. The short runway, surrounded by water, left little margin for error. Notorious wind conditions meant carrying enough fuel for multiple approach attempts while staying light enough for the landing constraints. Crosswinds often exceeded limits, requiring diversions.

I was very excited to see my friend as I hadn't seen in her in close to two years. My early arrival allowed me to analyse weather patterns, study wind forecasts, calculate optimal fuel loads. I printed documents for both of us, marking potential alternates if conditions deteriorated. Other pilots shared recent Hamilton Island experiences while I waited, 15 minutes before sign-on, still alone.

Sign on time is always an hour before push back, and my friend hadn't turned up yet. I sent her a text message but didn't get a response. I had printed out the briefing report so she wouldn't get caught being late for sign on. 15 minutes after sign-on she arrived. I waved, went up smiling and said, 'Hi! How's it going? I'm really excited we are going to be flying together today!'

She looked me up and down and said, 'How come you're flying with me? I'm meant to by flying with [male FO], I only spoke to him last night and he said he was excited to be flying with me. Where is he?'

My enthusiasm withered under her icy stare. Attempting recovery, I explained about the crew call.

'I don't know, I got a call from Crewing, and they asked me to do this. I thought it would be a great opportunity to catch up. It's been a couple of years, and you can fill me in on what's been happening,' I said quietly.

She turned away without saying a word, hair flicking dismissively, engaging another pilot in conversation.

I explained I had printed out the briefing report, the weather, and the flight plan, so everything was ready to go. I had made notes if she wanted to check them. She turned, snatched all the paperwork off me, ceremoniously threw them in the bin, then turned back and continued to talk to the male pilot on the other side. *She must be having a bad morning.*

I collected all my stuff and got ready to go to the aircraft. The company had a rule all pilots needed to be at the aircraft at minus 40, that is, 40 minutes before push back.

'I'll go to the aircraft and meet you there,' I told her.

'No. I'm the Captain. We leave when I say.' she responded.

I stood around talking to some people and waited for her to be ready. I checked the weather again and the fuel requirements in case anything had changed.

We reached the plane barely 25 minutes before pushback. Gate staff needed to report our tardiness. I smoothed things over, promising no delays. In the cockpit, I prepared everything for both roles while she chatted with cabin crew. Each checklist item dragged as she applied makeup and brushed her hair, taking precious minutes we didn't have.

At 5 minutes to push back she called for the pre-flight checklist. She was taking a long time to do everything, now putting on more lipstick and again brushing her hair. I needed to slow down to match her pace, thinking to myself, *that's fine, she's the Captain.*

We pushed back about 10 minutes late. We needed to radio in the reason after take-off. I made a note to do that.

We eventually got airborne, and as we climbed past 5,000 ft the auto pilot was engaged, the Captain proceeded to get jewellery out of her bag and put it on. Bracelets, earrings, necklace, and rings. The mirror came out and she started doing her eye make-up. We were still below 10,000 ft where there's a requirement to be a 'sterile' cockpit, meaning these types of distractions weren't allowed.

I stayed silent, which in hindsight I shouldn't have. I kept an eye out and was extra vigilant considering we were still climbing.

A large cloud was forming ahead of us, and I asked her if she would like me to radio in a request for a diversion around the cloud.

Without looking up, she said, 'No.'

She then looked up and said, 'Request divert 5 miles right of track due to weather.' I radioed in the diversion.

We had 60 seconds to divert, she took the full 60. We did the transition checklist, then she went back to her head down. She was only on heading select so our track (path) was getting wider and wider.

'Just confirming we are still in heading?' I asked.

'That's what I wanted,' was her terse reply, without looking up.

She then looked up and put it back in L-Nav V-Nav, which is following the planned track with the autopilot.

I started to worry that maybe her negative attitude was due to something I had done wrong, and started to question myself.

We got to cruise, and I tried to start a chat with her. 'How's it all going?' 'How have you been?' 'It's been so long since I've seen you.'

Everything I said was met with one-word answers, whilst she looked out the window. She then took out a book and started reading.

I kept doing my duties, writing down the numbers required as I was 'pilot not flying'. I got the weather for Hamilton Island and handed it to her. 'Get it again! I can't read it.' she said. I got it again, wrote the details in very clear writing, and handed it to her again.

She said, 'I can't read this, I'll just have to listen to it myself.' As she was listening, she was ticking off the weather I had written down, so she *could* read it after all.

The Hamilton Island approach demanded perfect timing. Too high or fast meant overshooting the runway. The landing came in hard, enough to pop overhead lockers. Passengers audibly murmured concerns during disembarking.

Throughout subsequent sectors, cockpit tension mounted. My attempts at conversation hit walls of monosyllables or silence. She challenged weather reports despite clearly understanding them, creating unnecessary stress during critical phases.

I did the walkaround and got everything ready. She hadn't told me, so when I came back in, I asked if I would be flying this next sector. She said 'No.' The pilot flying does less admin and radio, so it is the coveted role, plus you actually get to fly.

We took off again and it was a mostly silent flight back to Sydney. This was going to be a long day; we had another 2 sectors to go, and it really wasn't turning out to be the great day I had anticipated.

We landed in Sydney late, which was due to our original delayed departure out of Sydney, so we were now late departing for Maroochydore.

The passengers were boarding, and I noticed Dawn Fraser was on our flight. I had a 'fan girl' moment and told the Captain she was on board.

'I fly her all the time. She knows me. We are good friends,' she stated. 'I'm sick of getting photos with her all the time though.'

'When we land, I might see if I can get a photo and talk to her,' I said sheepishly.

'No. You will be busy,' she stated.

'Why?'

'You will be doing the walkaround and the pre-flight,' she replied.

On the flight to Maroochydore, I finally called it.

'There is all this tension. I'm not sure if this is something I have done, or you're not having a great day. Is there something going on in your life that I can help with?' I asked.

Her response was startling.

'I'm sick of you! I wish you would just shut up!' After some silence she continued, 'When you were pregnant, you couldn't help but to rub that in my face, and then when you had your twins! I don't care about your twins and that's all you want to talk about.'

I sat stunned. We hadn't spoken since her abortion. My mind raced. Had she confused me with someone else? Imagined conversations? She claimed I tried usurping her Captain's authority that morning. My apologies about helping, because she was late, only fuelled her anger.

'Get back in your box. You think you know everything, and you know nothing.'

I knew then, that there was something more going on. I fought back tears, focusing on clouds outside. Professional responsibilities kept me going. In Maroochydore, I did get my photo with Dawn Fraser. She was lovely.

The final sector stretched endlessly. Hostile silence made me question if I should continue the flight. I restricted myself to minimum required communication, every word measured carefully. This contradicted everything *good* cockpit resource management taught us. Open dialogue between pilots keeps flights safe. Respect facilitates vital information exchange. Without these, subtle warning signs might go unmentioned until too late.

After we landed, my farewell handshake met empty air. Walking through the terminal, professional composure finally cracked. In my car, tears flowed freely while I questioned every interaction, searching for mistakes. Her accusations about me flaunting my twins made *no* sense given our two-year lost contact.

I had walked into something that had gone on in her head, and unfortunately it wasn't the great day I had hoped for.

Other female pilots later shared similar experiences with her. Stories of competitive behaviour, cold shoulders, denied flying opportunities, and obvious male pilot preferences painted a disturbing pattern. These revelations saddened me because flying with other women usually brought such positive energy to the flight deck.

Most female pilots supported each other *fiercely*. We celebrated achievements, shared knowledge, and created informal mentoring networks. Many of us became close friends beyond work.

Now though, we no longer talked in the crew room, and whenever we did pass each other in the terminal, there was always something more interesting for us both to look at.

Fate reunited this difficult friendship months later through another crew scheduling call. Fear gripped me seeing her name as Captain. Should I call in sick? Make excuses? Following my core belief that things *always* work out, I drove to work despite the mounting anxiety.

The universe delivered *magnificently*. Minutes before reaching the airport, crewing called with changed plans. She had called in sick. I was asked if I would ferry an aircraft to New Zealand for maintenance and did I have my passport with me? 'Umm, YES!'

The day had started out looking like it wouldn't be great, but I had put it out there, that my day *was* going to work out, and it *did*.

This day transformed into pure adventure. International terminal excitement. Duty-free shopping between flight preparations. Learning new ferry flight procedures added professional growth to personal enjoyment. No passengers or cabin crew meant handling everything *ourselves*—from door operation to customs requirements. Each new task brought fresh challenges and satisfaction.

Buying emergency overnight supplies added unexpected fun to the journey. Christchurch welcomed me with its stunning beauty and warm hospitality. Morning dread had evolved into career-enriching opportunity. Life reinforced its lasting lesson again. *Trust your instincts*, face challenges directly, and remain open to unexpected joys.

That day reminded me why I love aviation. Beyond sophisticated machines and complex procedures lies something deeper.

Flying connects people, builds bridges, opens horizons. Whether facing difficult colleagues or tricky approaches, maintaining professionalism while staying true to yourself creates the foundation for lasting success.

Gluten Air Tolerance

Dating another pilot seemed perfect for balancing our complex schedules. Living in different states made time together precious, so we often bid for shared trips. Our romantic strategy landed us a four-day pairing, flying out of Perth, finishing with a Darwin–Sydney run. The perfect plan for maximizing our time together turned into an unexpected lesson in relationship humility.

That last day of our romantic pairing, was a flight to Darwin, a couple of hours in the airport, then the final sector back to Sydney. In Darwin airport I had some noodles from the food court.

Now, I have a dietary condition related to gluten which developed after chemotherapy treatment. Oh, how I miss croissants, baguettes, and real spaghetti!

At the time I was assured the noodles were gluten-free. They weren't.

The first warning signs appeared during pre-flight checks. My stomach started its uncomfortable expansion as we reached cruise altitude. Thankfully, my boyfriend took pilot flying duties while I handled radio calls and paperwork. The physics of high-altitude air pressure worked against me. Much like those innocent-looking chip packets that balloon at cruise level, my intestines staged their own expansion party.

Throughout the flight, my stomach was getting more and more uncomfortable. Then came descent.

I had zero control over the deflation, it had to escape my body somehow, and it started to come out. Until this point in our relationship, we had maintained that magical early-dating phase where bodily functions remained politely unacknowledged. That facade was about to spectacularly shatter.

The noxious aftermath of gluten betrayal created an invisible but potent presence in our shared cockpit. Fighting against nature proved futile. Doubled over in pain, trapped in the confines of the flight deck, I faced an impossible choice between professional dignity and physical agony.

There are air gaspers (air vents) on either side of the cockpit. Every pilot knows about the unspoken language of air gaspers: Moving your air vent to point across the cockpit sends a clear message about atmospheric conditions. My boyfriend slowly reached up and adjusted his gasper, aiming it deliberately in my direction. The gesture screamed volumes about the quality of air on his side of the flight deck. Mortified, I aligned my gasper with his, trying to create that invisible barrier between us.

The situation deteriorated further as we descended through 20,000 feet. My body's protests against the gluten betrayal became audible, penetrating even our noise-cancelling headphones. Communication was reduced to mandatory checklist items; his responses were clipped and minimal.

After landing, he abandoned standard shutdown procedures, cutting both engines simultaneously in his rush for fresh air. His head disappeared out the side window, supposedly checking with non-existent ground crew. The excuse fooled nobody.

Our planned romantic evening evaporated faster than the cabin air pressure. His sudden urgent need for sleep provided a transparent but welcome escape route for both of us. Looking back now, knowing what I *now* know about his philandering I wish I had eaten an even *bigger* serve of noodles!

(See next story...)

Keenly-Huntingcock and Melon Boobs

Cancer treatment had stripped me of more than just my hair—it had completely eroded my self-confidence. The acrimonious divorce that followed delivered additional blows, with cutting comments about my physical appearance driving the final nail into my self-esteem coffin. Pale and puffy, with sparse eyebrows, and patchy hair regrowth (resembling curly pubic hair), I felt plain and invisible.

My emotional fragility made me the perfect target for a manipulative narcissist.

He first appeared in the crew room—older, shorter, foppish and unattractive, with horrible teeth, and noticeably awkward. Yet his English accent and charming demeanour offered a salve for my wounded spirit. His romantic pursuit felt healing, making me feel desirable again after my cancer diagnosis. The long-distance relationship between NSW and Queensland seemed manageable, especially with his daily phone calls full of promises and sweet nothings.

He told elaborate stories painting him as a hero in every scene. A 'Super Pilot' and former SAS Green Beret who advised military hierarchy on warfare tactics. He regaled our colleagues with tales of his elite military service, even claiming possession of a special watch—pressing its secret button would summon an elite SAS rescue team, seemingly appearing from the sky to his aid. Remarkably, many fellow pilots believed these fantastical tales, testament to his masterful manipulation.

His residential arrangement should have raised red flags, but in my state I chose to ignore. His 'ex-wife' lived in another 'wing' of his 'estate'—caring for his dogs during his absences. I later discovered his palatial estate was a simple little house with no 'wings' to accommodate his 'ex-wife'. They still lived together. I was too enchanted by his attention to question anything. Each weekend, he'd return to Queensland, claiming his dogs needed him. He phoned me daily.

Eighteen months into our relationship, Facebook messages started arriving from random women. 'What are you doing with my man?!' accompanied by increasingly hostile comments and evidence of their relationship. He dismissed them all with practiced ease: 'She's a crazy ex.,' or 'She's a bunny boiler.' I trusted his explanations because he had become my emotional crutch, making me feel whole again.

The 'bunny boiler'—a world-renowned opera singer— persisted, sending lengthy messages and damning photographic evidence of their ongoing relationship.

Rather than questioning *him*, we two professionally successful women, the opera singer and me, engaged in a toxic competition, trying to outdo each other with tales of his devotion and gifts. We tallied presents, compared romantic gestures, and fought for his attention, like prizes in a meaningless contest. Daily Facebook updates became weapons in our arsenal, each trying to prove our *superior* claim to his affections. Recent photos emerged showing them together, despite her living in England. When intimate images followed, my anger finally found its voice.

Instead of directing my rage at him, I attacked her, parroting his dismissive labels. She called me, 'Michelle Huntingcock;' I retaliated with 'Melon Boobs,' mocking her appearance. Our petty warfare served his manipulation perfectly, distracting us from his deceptions. Cheekily, I embraced the name, styling myself as 'Michelle Keenly-Huntingcock' humorously adding an air of sophistication to the insult, *and* removing the sting. Our social media exchanges became increasingly bitter, each convinced the other was the enemy.

His manipulation followed a calculated pattern: love bombing followed by ghosting, creating emotional dependency through alternating attention and abandonment. He showered us with compliments, gifts, and sweet words, then disappeared, leaving us questioning our worth.

Just as doubt peaked, he'd return with renewed intensity and fresh promises. Each cycle deepened our emotional investment.

Everything came to a head when, on a flight, the cabin supervisor came into the flight deck all frazzled.

She said to the Captain I was flying with, 'I don't know what to do!'

'What's wrong?' the Captain asked.

'My boyfriend won't pay for an abortion,' she complained.

You guessed it: my narcissist boyfriend. I had started to wonder if the rumours about his wandering penis were true; this confirmed it.

This revelation spurred action. I reached out to every woman who'd contacted me, including his not-so-ex-wife, sharing my timeline with him and his lies about each of them. Eight women replied, each sharing similar stories. Later, we also discovered a *male* cabin crew member in his web of deception. All successful professionals —pilots, performers, business owners and cabin crew, each carrying private vulnerabilities he'd expertly exploited.

The opera singer and I finally acknowledged our misplaced anger. We'd competed for a prize not worth winning. As our communication evolved from hostile to healing, we discovered countless commonalities beyond our shared manipulator. Daily conversations revealed shared passions, similar life experiences, and complementary personalities.

Six months of increasingly deep friendship led to a bold decision—meeting in person, 'halfway' between London and Sydney. We decided Perth in Western Australia, would be the meeting place.

Our families, concerned about lingering animosity, listened anxiously on phone calls as we approached the hotel we had chosen. My parents insisted on staying on the line as I entered the hotel; her family did the same, all fearing the worst from this meeting of former rivals.

The tension broke instantly the door opened, revealing not an enemy but a soul sister. We'd shared the same pain, the same manipulation, the same healing journey. Years of manufactured competition melted away in an embrace that felt like coming home. We'd found in each other the genuine connection we'd sought in *him*.

Laughter replaced bitterness as we uncovered his countless deceptions: presents he'd regifted between us, recycled romantic gestures, and manufactured moments. A sunrise photo he'd sent me had actually been taken while she lay in his bed and photographed him taking it—a perfect metaphor for his layers of deceit. Each revelation strengthened our growing friendship.

From the ashes of manipulation rose an unshakeable friendship. While we suspect he continues his predatory pattern elsewhere, we emerged stronger, wiser, and enriched by a bond that transcended his toxic influence.

Sometimes life's deepest connections grow from shared wounds, and the best revenge is finding *joy* despite the pain.

Our story contains many more elements—revenge, his manipulative threats of self-harm, and darker moments—perhaps worthy of a screenplay, yet focusing on these aspects might feed the narcissism that nearly destroyed my friend and I, both.

Instead, we celebrate the unexpected gift of friendship forged in the flames of adversity.

Weird Captain

My journey to Captain's stripes took different paths at different airlines. At Regional Express (Rex), I moved from First Officer to Captain within just 2 years. Virgin Australia, being larger, demanded more patience. I was nine years wearing three stripes before my seniority number finally opened the door to command training.

The timing of my last flight as a First Officer proved memorable, though not in the way I had hoped! Hamilton Island loomed ahead, notorious among pilots for its challenging instrument approaches. Flying without visual references demands intense concentration—even in good conditions. The shortened runway, surrounded by water, leaves little room for error. It was a difficult landing at the best of times.

Below 10,000 feet, we maintain what we call a 'sterile cockpit'—no casual conversation, no distractions; only essential communication and checklists.

I had commenced the instrument approach, my mind focused entirely on the precise sequence of steps needed to guide our aircraft safely to the ground.

The Captain's voice shattered this concentration, 'I don't think you'll be a good Captain.'

His words hung in the air between us. *Why that statement? Why during one of the most demanding phases of flight?* The timing seemed deliberately chosen to undermine my confidence at a critical moment.

Rather than engage, I channelled my rising frustration into proving him wrong. Each movement of the controls became a statement. The aircraft descended smoothly on the perfect glide path; speed exactly as required. The touchdown emerged as one of my finest, the wheels kissing the runway precisely in the designated zone.

After we taxied to the Bay and shut down, I turned to him. 'Why did you say that to me, especially during landing?'

The countless hours of study flashed through my mind. Years spent mastering aircraft systems, company policies, engine management, regulations, and complex airspace requirements. My technical knowledge matched or exceeded what was needed for command.

His response dripped with prehistoric thinking, 'Don't worry, Michelle. It's not just you, I don't think any women make good Captains.'

He was right. Women don't make good Captains.

We make *great* Captains.

He was weird, and an asshole.

His chauvinistic attitude joined a long list of motivations and reasons why command training couldn't come *fast* enough for me. Each flight with pilots like him strengthened my resolve.

Their small-minded prejudices became fuel for the journey ahead.

Keep pushing forward. Keep proving them wrong.

Keep going until you can't.

Part 8 Virgin Captain

Captain Michelle Huntington

I Made Magda Cry

The day I became a Captain, I also thanked an Australian comedy legend.

Magda Szubanski—you make me laugh till I cry! The star of TV's 'Full Frontal', 'Fast Forward', 'Kath and Kim', and the movie 'Babe,' had touched millions of Aussies with her humour. Now she was on my flight, during one of my most significant professional moments.

This was my final command upgrade sector, the last test flight before earning my fourth stripe. The check Captain (the assessor), sat behind the first officer and myself. We'd prepared the aircraft for departure and passengers were boarding, then I spotted her. Magda Szubanski walking down the aerobridge.

My heart raced. The fan in me wanted to reach out, while the professional Captain-in-Training maintained composure. I turned to my check Captain, who had already assured me I would pass, (unless I fucked up this last leg, a distinct possibility,) but I couldn't miss this opportunity.

'Would it be alright if I welcomed her?' I asked.

His warm response gave me permission, 'Of course. Go welcome her.'

I had created postcards featuring a terrible aviation joke.

What's a Pilot's favourite flavoured chip?

The back displayed a caricature of me with the answer: *Plane!*

Grabbing one, I wrote a quick message.

Dear Magda, thank you for making a nation laugh, and for being you.

I signed it, *Captain Michelle*. Perhaps tempting fate before officially earning the title.

Walking to her seat, I crouched down beside her.

'I just wanted to say I really admire you for your work, as an actor, a comedian and making us laugh. I've admired you for years, and it's my pleasure to fly you as the Captain on this flight to Brisbane,' I said with goosebumps on my arms.

She took the card, reading it silently. Tears welled in her eyes before she could speak. A quiet 'Thank you' carried more weight than a thousand words. I touched her hand gently before returning to the flight deck.

Standing in the cockpit, I made myself a promise. I would make this the *best* flight she had experienced. Not just because she was Magda, but because this flight marked my transition to Captain. Both of us sharing an unexpectedly emotional moment.

I passed my check ride. The day I became a Captain, I also thanked an Australian legend. Bloody beautiful.

Fangirl

Many famous people fly just like everyone else and not in a private jet. My encounters with them brought out my inner fangirl more times than I care to admit.

Leather in the Air

We were the first early morning flight out of Adelaide, and it was expected to be routine. During my walkaround, multiple guitar cases caught my attention, sparking curiosity about which band might be on our flight. Adelaide's fishbowl aerobridge offered a perfect vantage point from the cockpit. My professional demeanour crumbled instantly when I spotted her. Unable to contain my excitement, I waved enthusiastically, grinning like a starstruck teenager. She waved back.

Dressed all in leather, wearing dark sunglasses, and radiating pure rock star energy, my childhood idol from 'Happy Days', Leather Tuscadero, aka Suzi Quatro, strode toward our aircraft. She visited the cockpit while I gushed embarrassingly. Rock stars truly carry a unique presence. She posed for photos, touched my arm affectionately, transforming an ordinary morning into an unforgettable memory.

Don't Look At Me

I got the call that we had a private charter on a 737. Hiring an entire commercial aircraft usually meant someone significant. The instructions came down from the top. A very famous passenger needed transport from Sydney to Perth, requesting complete privacy. No disturbances. No looking.

'Come on, who is it?' My curiosity got the better of me.

'We have been asked to keep it private,' was the response from the senior base pilot.

'All I have to do is look at the passenger manifest and I'll know. Come on, who?' I pushed. He wouldn't say, but the manifest did.

You were another of my musical heroes growing up and you may have been Born to Run, but baby I was Born to Fly. I hope you enjoyed your smooth flight and perfect landing. You're welcome.

The Naturalist

Pre-flight preparations paused for a special pre-boarding passenger. I can't recall where we were flying, maybe it was Brisbane. His familiar face appeared in the aerobridge, bringing unexpected delight. This time without checking the manifest, excitement overwhelmed my professional reserve.

'Oh my goodness, look who it is!' I exclaimed to our younger cabin supervisor.

She replied,

'Who?'

As Sir David Attenborough stepped aboard, I gestured excitedly, 'This is Sir David Attenborough. He is the most lovely man, and world renowned naturist.'

Sir David looked at me and burst out laughing, while his travel companion shook her head.

I was *fangirling* big time.

'Oh no, wait!'

In my excitement, I had managed to call the legendary Sir David Attenborough a nudist.

Girls in the Box Office

Female pilots remained rare during my early years, leaving few role models beyond Amelia Earhart with her cautionary tale. Julia Gillard's rise to become Australia's first female Prime Minister expanded young girls' possibilities, adding political leadership to their vocabulary of potential future careers.

During her book tour, we flew Julia to Tasmania. Upon learning both Captain and First Officer were female, she requested a cockpit visit.

Many people don't know this but when the cockpit has two female pilots, it's called a Box Office, not a cockpit.

On landing, we welcomed Julia up front and celebrated female leadership, with a photo of course.

Fly or Swim

There are many other famous people I have flown but the lady that will finish this chapter deserves the final story. She is very famous in Australia for her sporting achievements, however it's the way she behaves on my flights that I respect.

Being instantly recognisable, she gets a lot of attention from crew and passengers alike. She is always the last one to leave the flight because she never declines a request for a photo or autograph.

She is the famous and humble and Dawn Fraser: Not only are you an Australian legend, you were always an absolute pleasure to fly.

I Turn Left

Female pilots can sometimes confuse people. After years of flying, certain moments stand out, bringing unexpected humour to our professional world.

After the pre-flight walkaround, the aerobridge often proved highly entertaining. Passengers, territorial about their boarding positions, would unconsciously or consciously block the path, determined not to let anyone pass them. Many times, absorbed in their own worlds, they'd physically prevent me from passing, only to turn and spot my uniform. Their stammered apologies usually drew my standard response: 'It doesn't matter, we are not going anywhere until I'm on the plane anyway.'

Flying regularly meant developing relationships with crew members, both familiar faces and new ones joining the team.

One particular flight brought a memorable encounter. Approaching the front door in full Captain uniform, a new flight attendant politely requested my boarding pass.

I tried lightening the moment with a gentle joke, 'It's OK, I turn left.'

First-day nerves and excitement can blur even the most obvious appearance. My smile and reference to entering the cockpit failed to register. She turned anxiously to her colleague, reporting, 'This person doesn't have a boarding pass.'

When it was pointed out to her that my uniform indicated I would be *flying the plane*, her mortified apology only made the moment even more endearing.

This next story was quite the funny sight.

After landing in Melbourne, passengers were starting to disembark. I was standing at the cockpit door, thanking the departing passengers as usual, when I witnessed a domino effect of human surprise. Passengers typically rush toward freedom, building momentum as they near the exit.

One gentleman, noticing the Captain saying farewell, processed my gender with such shock he stopped dead in his tracks. His abrupt halt and loud exclamation, 'The Captain's a chick!' created a chain reaction: behind him, following passengers collided with his stationary frame, tumbling backward into each other like human dominoes!

PILC

A Sydney to Mackay flight started unusually. Two plain-clothed detectives escorted a young man aboard, a jacket concealing his handcuffed hands. A PILC (Prisoner In Legal Custody), returning for a court hearing. Standard protocol required advance notification to the Captain.

The PILC took his assigned seat at the rear before regular passenger boarding commenced. My First Officer was having his first flight after being 'checked to line'.

Fresh from intensive training, these pilots typically demonstrate exceptional standards, though understandable anxiety about flying with unfamiliar captains often accompanies them.

Wanting to build his confidence, I offered him choice of sectors. He opted to fly to Mackay, a smart decision allowing me to manage the flight, whilst he handled the controls.

His take off was good and solid, and we chatted on our way up to Mackay. Air traffic control typically guides us by telling us what to do and where to go in relation to other aircraft, effectively holding our hand. The approach to Mackay involved a specific procedure, after leaving controlled airspace. Without air traffic control's guiding hand, complexity increased. The First Officer requested to hand-fly the circuit and approach. We briefed thoroughly in preparation.

Local area traffic control had just taken over when cabin alert chimes broke our concentration. These emergency signals rarely replace standard intercom communication. I was able to contact the Cabin Supervisor on the intercom and received a brief on what was happening. I asked her to come into the flight deck to discuss.

Instructing the First Officer to commence descent, I notified air traffic control of our intentions before receiving full details. The situation in the cabin had escalated rapidly. The PILC had violently attacked both detectives, breaking one's nose with his elbow before attempting the same with the second. His legs had smashed the seat ahead, throwing its occupant forward. Blood covered the cabin, passengers showed extreme distress, though additional restraints now secured the prisoner.

The Cabin Supervisor assured me immediate intervention wasn't required. Relocated passengers appeared unharmed. I requested continued assessment of both crew and passenger welfare.

I asked for her to return to the cabin, and make a further assessment to ensure both cabin crew and passengers were OK.

Our landing needed expediting. Taking control at 10,000 feet, I activated seatbelt signs and announced preparations for arrival. I notified air traffic control about requiring Australian Federal Police assistance, explaining our contained but serious situation. Medical support would be needed to address potential injuries.

Mackay granted priority a landing with direct approach. I re-briefed the First Officer on the revised procedure, explaining his radio responsibilities while I flew. Ground support would likely include police, ambulance, and fire services. The FO would now be the pilot not flying and would be doing the radios.

I informed the cabin supervisor that once we landed, I would leave the seatbelt sign on and make a PA to the passengers. The police would board via the rear stairs to disembark the PILC. There would also be guest services on arrival for any passengers that required assistance.

Everyone was now informed. We landed and taxied to the bay to be met by a full contingent of police, ambulance and the fire brigade.

Post-landing instructions kept passengers seated while police removed our uncooperative prisoner via the rear stairs. He resisted, resulting in a few missed stairs on the way down. Passengers applauded both police and cabin crew intervention.

I let the passengers know that they could talk to myself, the cabin supervisor, or guest services if they had anything they needed to discuss.

Extensive paperwork and cabin cleaning followed. A crucial debrief with cabin crew explored their emotional readiness for return flights. I provided direct contact numbers and assured them of company support.

We somehow achieved on-time departure despite the chaos. Airborne again, my quiet First Officer finally spoke. 'Wow, is that what usually happens?'

'No,' I laughed, 'that was not a normal flight.'

Karen in Row 3

Safety briefings form a critical part of every flight, for good reason. Consider *why* we repeat it every single flight. While frequent flyers might tune out, interrupting this vital procedure crosses a firm line.

Our Sunshine Coast flight carried its typical mix. Holidaymakers dreaming of golden beaches; business travellers scanning laptops; families wrangling excited children. One group of women had clearly started their celebrations early, their pre-flight drinks fuelling their rising volume levels.

During our live safety demonstration, Karen in row 3 decided her cross-aisle conversation warranted more attention than potential life-saving information. A gentle request from our cabin crew to pause her chat met brief compliance, before she resumed shouting to her friends, leaning across our crew member mid-demonstration.

The second request for her to 'Shhh' was met with a 'Who are you to tell me to shhhhh?!'

The Cabin Supervisor had observed the situation and interrupted the safety briefing by announcing over the PA, 'Ladies and Gentlemen, my apologies for interrupting the safety demonstration, but we will have to pause to attend to a situation.' A whole plane load of passengers now craned their necks to see what was happening up at row 3.

A call to the flight deck detailed the disruption. I asked if they would like me to come out and provide assistance. This is why we call our Cabin Supervisors, 'Cabin Captains'. He told me he had the situation handled, and not to worry. I had complete faith in him.

Karen received an invitation to the front of the aircraft. The opened door provided her swift exit from our flight. Her friends, perhaps secretly relieved, continued their journey without her, their Queensland lunch plans likely improved by her absence.

Sorry Karen, passenger safety outweighs your social calendar every time.

Risk 185 or Save 1?

Making life and death decisions demands separation from your human emotions. Our training emphasises rational thinking. With 185 lives behind the flight door, closing that door helps create the mental space needed to make difficult choices.

Simulator training regularly challenged us with scenarios that pitted individual needs against group safety. A common simulation involved departing before dangerous weather, then facing a medical emergency. While ground-based instincts push toward helping individuals, altitude changes everything.

We have cabin crew who are medically trained, and in such situations a call would go out to see if any passengers could also provide medical assistance.

The flight deck maintains contact with ground-based doctors for guidance about optimal care on board and in their destinations. However, our training speaks clearly. While we do *everything* possible to help in medical emergencies, we never risk the entire aircraft's safety for one person.

The math sounds cold. Do you risk 185 lives to save one?

This principle faced real-world testing over the Great Australian Bight, midway through a Sydney–Perth flight. That route requires you to always be within a certain distance of a suitable aerodrome based on fuel, weather, or even the ability to fly with one engine.

We were at cruising height, when we got a call. Cabin crew reported a passenger struggling with breathing, panic attacks, and concerning symptoms indicating Deep Vein Thrombosis (DVT). Her pale, clammy appearance suggested serious distress.

Our first trained response, "sit on our hands," means assessing before acting, gathering information without emotional responses. In these situations, we rely on the NITS protocol:

- Nature – Understanding exactly what's happening
- Intent – Determining our planned course of action
- Time – Establishing timeline for significant actions
- Special Circumstances – Identifying unusual factors like oxygen requirements or emergency services

The Cabin Supervisor's unusual agitation caught my attention. Questions received incomplete answers, her emotional state escalating with each passenger interaction. Later we learned about her own previous experience. A private flight on which her passenger died from DVT had triggered post-traumatic stress.

Recognising her compromised state, we requested a volunteer from the existing crew to assume her role. A crew member with prior medical training stepped up, coordinating with an onboard doctor and paramedic, while maintaining clear communication with the flight deck. Their medical backgrounds proved invaluable for assessing our situation.

Our options needed careful evaluation. Adelaide offered full facilities but required significant deviation from our flight path. Forrest airfield presented serious limitations, lacking aircraft stairs and promising no ground staff for over an hour after arrival. Perth, our destination, lay ahead. Multiple attempts at radio medical consultation failed through both HF and VHF frequencies, leaving the decision squarely in our hands.

I transferred aircraft control to my First Officer and analysed our choices. Conflicting medical advice complicated matters. The paramedic recommended elevating the passenger's legs while the doctor advised against it. Our onboard medical manuals agreed with the doctor's recommendation.

We were approaching the point where it would be quicker to continue onto Perth than to divert. I had to make the decision.

Moving to the rear galley, I found our passenger much improved, having juice and a sandwich. While talking to her, immediate travel history revealed continuous flights from New York through Los Angeles and then Sydney, with minimal ground time between connections. Probable dehydration emerged as a contributing factor. After presenting all options, including ambulance services in Adelaide, limited support in Forrest, or continuing to Perth, she chose Perth.

Consulting both medical professionals about descent considerations, I implemented their recommendations. I discussed everything with the FO and radioed ahead to Perth requesting a cruise descent, where we start our descent a lot further out. Instead of descending at 2,000 feet per minute, we were going to descend at 500 feet per minute.

Any other passengers who may have had a cold or blocked sinus also benefited from the cabin pressure reducing more slowly.

We maintained constant communication with the cabin crew, ensuring they could update the passenger on our progress and estimated arrival time. The flight's end point helped manage her anxiety levels. Priority landing clearance and paramedic reception arrangements brought us in 10 minutes ahead of schedule.

Despite our preparations for rear door medical evacuation, she declined assistance and walked off normally with other passengers.

We never received follow-up about her condition, but the incident reinforced our emergency response protocols.

That day offered clear options without weather complications, making the decision process straightforward. Different conditions might have forced harder choices. Heavy weather at diversion airports, minimum fuel scenarios, or deteriorating patient conditions would have significantly complicated our options. The principle stands though. We never risk 185 lives to save one. Safety remains paramount in every decision.

These situations test our training, demanding quick analysis and decisive action while maintaining emotional distance. The structured approach, from the NITS protocol through descent planning, provides a critical framework for managing medical emergencies at altitude.

Each decision must balance individual needs against overall flight safety, always remembering our responsibility to every soul on board.

Flying isn't just about reacting; it's thinking three steps ahead, planning meticulously so when surprises come, and they always do, you're already prepared.

Innuendos

In my aviation career, many innuendos arose tied to my gender. While I appreciate good humour, a clear distinction exists between laughing *with* someone, and laughing *at* them.

Early in my career, flying a medical run through outback Australia, sinus pressure wreaked havoc with my ears. Constant Mintie chewing failed to clear the blockage. During approach, I attempted radio contact, pushing the lolly into my cheek to speak clearly. My garbled transmission prompted an apology.

'I'm sorry. I've got my mouth full,' I apologised.

'I'll bet you do.' was the response.

Another time, approaching King Island, my routine radio call received an unexpected response from another pilot who had just landed.

'I didn't realise they let flight attendants do the radio.'

After we landed, the same pilot came over to the aircraft and asked to sit in the cockpit.

'No,' was my resounding response.

On a different flight, discussing runway requirements with air traffic control proved entertaining.

'We could take the full length,' I requested.

'I bet you can,' came the response.

That one amused me. Humour lands differently, depending on delivery. Laugh with me: *absolutely fine*. Mock from a position of imagined superiority: *absolutely not*.

These exchanges reflect broader industry attitudes. Each quip, while seemingly harmless, carried undertones of gender bias. Small moments accumulate, creating an environment where female pilots constantly navigate more than just aircraft.

We handle complex flight operations while fielding commentary our male colleagues *never* face.

Professional competence speaks louder than clever comebacks. My responses focused on maintaining dignity while demonstrating expertise.

Each successful flight, perfect landing, and managed challenge pushed back against outdated attitudes more effectively than words ever could.

Grabbed from Behind

Writing this chapter proved the most difficult for me. This story marked the end of my aviation career.

Pride filled me that morning preparing for my Sydney to Melbourne flight. My childhood dreams of becoming a pilot had materialised into reality. I had flown millions of passengers, millions of miles. As an Airline Captain, my complete dedication to aviation had earned the four stripes on my epaulettes.

As I was getting the flight ready, four very senior male Captains boarded my plane early, hitching a ride to Melbourne. I recognised them all, considering one a close friend.

The familiar scent of Jet A1 accompanied my walkaround inspection. Aircraft engines roared around me, their sound still thrilling after all these years. This was home. Standing on the tarmac, mentally checking pre-flight procedures, I felt complete certainty in my profession.

I walked up the rear stairs into the aircraft, greeting cabin crew, then walked forward through the cabin focused entirely on flight preparations. Then reality shattered.

WHAT THE FUCK!

My mind screamed as I passed the four Captains. One of them had reached between my legs and grabbed my crotch.

I spun around. 'What the fuck? Who did that?'

Silence met my question. I repeated myself, louder, 'Who did that?'

No one would meet my eye, though one visibly smirked. Complete shock propelled me forward toward the flight deck.

I went into overdrive. My racing mind catalogued every compromise made to fit their mould. What had I done to deserve this? I had done EVERYTHING they asked of me to become accepted in their boys' club. I had been told to not wear lipstick; don't smile; don't laugh; don't be too girly; don't say please and thank you when commanding the aircraft; don't wear your hair out; don't wear pink; and MAN UP.

Years spent conforming to their expectations of what makes a proper pilot. All that effort to join their club led to this violation.

I continued my walk to the flight deck. My mouth was dry. My heart was racing. Then a very painful memory overtook my thinking. Being grabbed had reminded me of a suppressed memory from years earlier.

I was 14 years old, attending a party with a friend. She and I naively accepted the copious amounts of alcohol our barman was plying us with at the party. His plan worked. On the walk home, in our inebriated state, he raped us both.

My teenage mind had buried that trauma, shouldering undeserved shame and responsibility. I never told *anyone*.

That painful distant memory, and the shock of what just happened in the aircraft aisle, overwhelmed my thoughts. Shock overwhelmed professional focus. My hands shook uncontrollably. Tears threatened. The complex task of readying a 737 for departure disappeared beneath waves of distress.

'Would you like a coffee?' the cabin supervisor asked as he entered the flight deck.

His routine question anchored me to reality. Captain's stripes meant responsibility. This behaviour demanded a response.

I am the Captain of this aircraft, I thought to myself. *I don't deserve this, and I am in charge here!*

I walked back down the aisle to the feeble four.

I demanded again, 'Who did it?'

Continued silence.

'OK, it's your choice. It's one off or four off.'

All four of them stood up, collected their things, and disembarked the aircraft.

The Captain, who I had considered a friend, turned to me, and said, 'You will regret this.'

Boys Will Be Boys

I was in complete shock.

I had just asked four Captains to leave my plane. None of them owned up to what had just happened. None of them had the balls to confront their fellow Captain who had just grabbed me on my vagina. None of them were man enough to show strength. Every cowardly one of them walked off that plane a smaller human being.

Every one of them had an opportunity to do the right thing and show integrity, to show other men, what *true* men would do, in that situation. *None* of them did. Not even my friend who had warned me with, 'You will regret this.'

Small men, with big egos, and no integrity. None.

They left the plane, and I called operations to inform them that I had removed the four.

When they asked why I had removed them from my flight. I simply said, 'it's personal.'

I was informed that they needed to be on the plane as they were travelling to Melbourne to start their own flights. I repeated, they weren't welcome on my plane.

I was stood down as Captain of that flight.

I walked off the plane and later spoke with my base manager.

He said I had to take it to HR. I did.

HR said I needed to write a report. I did.

I submitted my report with no response.

I asked my base manager what was happening with what I reported, and he said, 'If you don't hear anything then that's good news.' *How was I the one in trouble? If I don't hear anything back that's good news?! What the actual fuck?!*

Flying resumed but everything had changed. Their boys' club transformed into hostile territory. Despite my proven competence as Captain, coordinated efforts emerged to discredit and remove me.

HR is meant to be your safe place. The people who will have your back. You go to them when you need support, so that the injustices occurring can be dealt with aplomb and fairness. That wrongs will be *righted*.

Months later, questioning HR about my report produced an unconscionable response: 'Boys will be boys.'

The Chief Pilot, who was present for their dismissal of the seriousness, offered empty words. 'If you think that was an issue, then you should raise it with HR.'

'I did raise it with HR, and you just heard her response!' I fumed.

His diplomatic dodge followed. 'Well, if you want us to investigate this further, then we will do that.'

My fierce loyalty to the company crumbled. Twelve Christmases away from my family, never hesitating to support our aviation community, meant *nothing*.

Simulator checks I'd previously excelled at, became anxiety filled assessments, with the outcome dependant on who was checking me.

They demoted me, likely calculating future liability.

A union representative warned me clearly. 'They are going to get rid of you somehow.' They encouraged me to fight back.

I tried adapting to this new reality. My pattern of bending to accommodate, pushing through difficulties, reached its limit. My mantra, *Keep going until you can't* finally found its boundary. My mental and physical health, already tested by breast cancer, demanded priority.

COVID-19's arrival temporarily grounded flights. Virgin Australia entered administration, offering redundancies. Despite previous gratitude for their support during cancer treatment and opportunities to achieve childhood dreams, reality sank in.

Companies consist of *people*. Most proved amazing. Some destroyed everything.

Rather than continue to fight for my position, I walked away.

My dream job ended, leading toward unknown adventures. The aftermath rippled through the female pilot community. Several reached out privately, sharing similar experiences they'd never reported, fearing the same institutional betrayal. Their stories revealed a pattern. Most chose silence to protect their careers, watching another generation of female pilots face the same challenges they'd endured.

The industry's toxic culture thrived behind progressive publicity campaigns celebrating female pilots. While companies proudly advertised their commitment to gender equality, the reality in crew rooms and cockpits told a very different story. Male pilots who spoke up faced ostracism, and were labelled troublemakers for supporting female colleagues.

This environment encouraged silence, protected aggressive predators, and perpetuated discrimination.

My departure prompted quiet conversations among remaining female pilots. Some reconsidered their career choices, others developed elaborate strategies to avoid flying with certain males. Young women entering the profession still received warnings about specific pilots, passed through whisper networks that shouldn't need to exist.

The cost extends beyond individual careers. Airlines lose experienced pilots while maintaining systems that protect harassers.

Each departure represents years of training, experience, and expertise lost to a culture resistant to change. My story became cautionary—not about the risks of speaking up, but about the industry's failure to evolve.

Aviation gave me incredible experiences, but institutional failure to address sexual assault cost them an experienced Captain. More importantly, it preserved a culture where future female pilots face similar battles.

My departure opened a new chapter for me, however the industry's story remains unchanged until those with power choose *real* change over comfortable complicity with appallingly low professional and interpersonal standards.

Another adventure.

But to where?

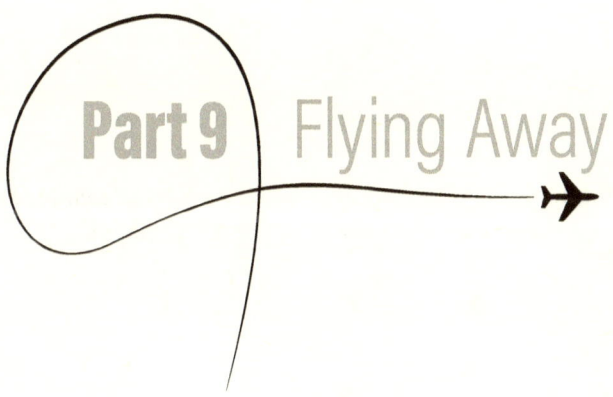

Part 9   Flying Away

'Success is not final, failure is not fatal: it is the courage to continue that counts.' - Winston Churchill

Flying Away

At first, I felt relief wash over me. Pure, *delicious* freedom. No more rosters, no more early starts, no more missing family events. I could sleep in, make my own schedule, live life on my terms.

Then it wasn't.

I experienced what I now know as Ego Death.

If I wasn't an Airline Captain anymore, who was I?

The question haunted me as my identity crumbled. It hit me like a punch in the gut, and I started to break down.

I spent way too much time in bed crying, doing online shopping that I couldn't afford, and drinking to numb the pain.

When your ego is dying the world becomes a confusing swirl. Nothing makes sense anymore. I was angry at the injustice, sad about losing my dream, disappointed in myself for walking away, and bone-deep exhausted from it all.

The growing financial stress twisted together with the shame of losing what I thought *defined* me, creating a spiral I couldn't escape.

It wasn't until my beautiful young daughter, my eternal optimist, came into my bedroom and innocently asked, 'Why do you cry all the time Mum? We love having you home.'

Those simple words cut through *everything*.

I got out of bed. I hugged her tight, and I started the rebuild.

I realised something important then. I didn't walk out on my love of aviation; I had left a toxic work environment. There's a world of difference.

Everything I had done in life had contributed a skill to my toolkit. My toolkit was overflowing: I can paint; I can weld; I can teach; I can solve complex problems; I can remain calm under pressure; I can negotiate; I can mentor; I can learn; I can study; I can understand the intricate nuances of human beings. My toolkit is full.

Looking back, I understood the weight I'd carried as one of only 500 female airline captains worldwide. Every flight deck entry brought scrutiny. Every decision, landing, and radio call seemed to represent not just my capabilities but the potential of *all* female pilots. That pressure to perform perfectly fed constant doubts, whispering questions about whether I truly belonged up there with those four stripes.

I had tried blending in at first, suppressing my natural style to mirror what I thought a Captain should be. Many pioneers learn this lesson. Blending in doesn't create change. It just maintains the barriers we're trying to break.

Since ending my career in aviation, my path has opened in unexpected ways. I helped a training business become a registered training organisation (RTO). I was employee number two in a tech start up that disrupted the early childcare market. I delivered a TEDx talk on a subject close to my heart: mindset. I became an 'artist in residence'. I now co-host a podcast: 'Captain and the Clown'. I am a Keynote Speaker, Corporate Trainer, Coach and Mentor, and my path forward is wide open.

Our identities grow through stories, shaped by moments when challenges force choices and create new directions. These crossroads define not just who we are, but how we lead. Being the only woman in the room once felt like a burden. Now I recognise it as an opportunity to show what's possible.

Post-traumatic growth only becomes visible in hindsight. When tears cloud your vision, seeing beyond immediate pain feels impossible.

Resilience isn't about bouncing back to what *was*. It's about bouncing *forward* into what could be.

The flexibility to move with life's turbulence while maintaining upward momentum comes from the stories *we tell ourselves*.

To own your narrative means taking pride in every chapter, even the painful ones. Leadership isn't about fitting existing moulds, but creating new spaces where everyone can thrive. Every experience, every setback, every triumph adds to the unique perspective we bring to each new challenge.

Here's what I now know. Your worst moments can become your best teachers. Your differences can become your superpowers. Your 'failures' can launch your greatest successes. That toxic workplace you left might just push you toward your true path.

In aviation, we learn that turbulence, while uncomfortable, often leads to clearer skies. Life proves similar. By embracing our complete stories, by sharing our authentic journeys, we don't just inspire change; we *become* it.

Your story isn't finished when one chapter ends—it's just getting interesting. Every skill you've gained, every challenge you've faced, every obstacle you've overcome—they're all preparing you for what's next.

I'm not an Airline Captain anymore. I'm something actually better. I'm me.

The sky isn't the limit.

It never was.

It's just the beginning.

Epilogue

When everything seems to be going against you, remember that the airplane takes off against the wind, not with the wind.

—Henry Ford

After all that happened, and with the gift of time, a model for how I approached challenges became clear.

SOAR—Finding Lift in Life's Challenges

In aviation, a headwind is crucial for take-off. It might seem counterintuitive: Why would you want wind pushing *against* your aircraft? That opposing force reduces the ground roll needed for take-off, increases your rate of climb, and improves overall aircraft performance. Without adequate headwind, you need more runway and more power to achieve the same result.

I've learned that life works in a similar way. Those forces that seem to oppose us often provide the resistance we need to lift off. Just as a bird can't soar without wind beneath its wings, we often can't rise to our full potential without facing and using the challenges that come our way.

Flying has taught me that life's most challenging moments often bring the most valuable lessons. Over thousands of hours working in the cockpit, I noticed a pattern in how successful pilots handle unexpected situations. Whether facing a lightning strike at night, managing difficult passengers, or navigating through severe weather, four key elements in their approach consistently emerged.

I call it **SOAR**.

Stop and Breathe.

When you hit unexpected turbulence, your first instinct might be to react immediately. Don't. Take a moment. Centre yourself. In that lightning strike over the Snowies, my initial impulse was to descend immediately. Instead, I paused, steadied my breathing, and assessed my situation. Those few seconds of clarity made all the difference. Just like using trim to stabilise an aircraft, taking that moment to steady yourself is the difference between a controlled, measured response and a knee-jerk reaction.

Observe.

Look at your situation objectively. What's really happening? What resources do you have? What can you control? During that flight with unruly passengers, observation revealed that the situation would only worsen unless we diverted. On another occasion, when all my instruments failed, careful observation of my surroundings and remembering my ground features helped me navigate safely home. Understanding your reality—not what you wish it was—is crucial for making sound decisions.

Adjust.

Based on your observations, modify your approach. When I was training in Wagga Wagga, being away from my son wasn't working. Rather than stubbornly pushing through,

I adjusted, finding ways to make the situation manageable until a transfer became possible. Similarly, when facing strong crosswinds, we adjust our approach angle and technique. The headwind isn't going away, but you can change how you *face* it.

Rise.

This is where you transform challenge into opportunity. Use that headwind to lift you higher. When I discovered the Piper Chieftain's limitations during that storm, it motivated me to pursue larger aircraft. Every obstacle became a stepping stone to something better. Just as pilots use rising air currents to gain altitude, we can use life's challenges to reach new heights.

SOAR isn't just about managing crises. It's about approaching life's challenges with the same methodical focus we use in aviation.

Take my experience instructing students. Initially, each new challenge—whether it was a student freezing at the controls, or misunderstanding a critical concept—seemed daunting. By applying SOAR principles, these challenges became opportunities to develop better teaching methods.

The method works because it mirrors how we naturally handle challenges when we're at our best. Just as pilots calculate their take-off performance considering wind conditions, we need to assess our situation before taking action. When that drunk passenger threw a bottle at my head, stopping to breathe gave me time to consider all options, rather than reacting emotionally. The observation phase revealed multiple issues—not just the immediate safety concern, but also the broader risk to the aircraft. Adjusting meant declaring an emergency and diverting, while Rising meant turning a potentially dangerous situation into a learning experience.

In the cockpit, we have checklists for everything. SOAR is like a mini checklist for life's turbulent moments. It doesn't guarantee perfect outcomes, but it helps ensure we're making decisions based on *clarity* rather than reaction. During my early charter days, flying that old Metroliner without autopilot taught me that sometimes the hardest conditions create the best learning environments. The constant trim adjustments and manual flying made me a better pilot for when I moved to larger aircraft.

Consider crosswind landings—they're often seen as challenging, but they teach us valuable lessons about control and adaptation. Similarly, life's crosswinds might push us off course, but they also teach us how to maintain our heading while adjusting to conditions. During my time teaching welding to apprentices, I learned that the best way to handle resistance wasn't to fight it, but to work *with it*, just like using a headwind for better performance.

The beauty of SOAR lies in its adaptability. Whether you're handling an engine failure at night or navigating a difficult conversation, the principles remain the same.

Stop, breathe, and avoid that initial panic response.

Observe your situation clearly, just as you'd scan your instruments in limited visibility.

Adjust your approach based on what you've observed, like choosing an alternate airport when weather deteriorates.

Finally, **Rise** above the challenge by learning from it and using it to improve.

I've seen pilots with thousands of flying hours make poor decisions because they rushed their response to a situation. I've also seen relatively inexperienced pilots handle complex situations beautifully because they took that crucial moment to stop and think. The difference wasn't in their flying skills but in their *approach* to the challenge.

Remember that time in Lake Cargelligo when my aircraft broke down? The entire community came together to help create a solution. By following what would later become my SOAR method, we turned a potential disaster into a triumph of ingenuity and community spirit.

SOAR evolved from countless moments in the air where critical success or failure hinged not on the challenge itself but on *how it was approached*. Each element emerged from real experiences: the calm after stopping to breathe during emergencies, the clarity that comes from careful observation, the power of adjusting approach rather than forcing a solution, and the growth that follows rising above difficulties.

Whether you're facing a technical emergency at altitude or a personal challenge on the ground, these principles apply. **Stop. Observe. Adjust. Rise**. Let each headwind become your lifting force.

In the end, SOAR isn't just a method—it's a mindset. It's about recognising that those forces pushing against us might just be *exactly* what we need. Sometimes the longest runway isn't as valuable as a good headwind.

'What the caterpillar calls the end of the world, the master calls a butterfly.' - Richard Bach

www.ingramcontent.com/pod-product-compliance
Lightning Source LLC
Chambersburg PA
CBHW020525080526
44583CB00013B/738